Romney Marsh

My Romney Marsh pictures are for Annie,
Sara, Joanna and Zack.
and in memory of John Soudain
With love

Romney Marsh

photographs by **Fay Godwin**

written by **Richard Ingrams**

Wildwood House London

First published in Great Britain 1980

Wildwood House Limited
1 Prince of Wales Passage
117 Hampstead Road
London NW1 3EE

Text copyright © 1980 Richard Ingrams
Photographs copyright © 1980 Fay Godwin

Designed by Ken Garland Associates
Maps drawn by Colin Bailey
Photographic prints made by Tom Ang

ISBN 0 7045 3039 2

Typeset by Inforum Ltd, Portsmouth
Printed and bound in Great Britain by
Biddles Ltd, Guildford

Contents

	General Map	6
	Introduction	8
Part One	Pett Level and the way to Rye	12
Part Two	Marsh and Canal to Hythe	56
Part Three	The Shore to Dungeness and beyond	138
	Bibliography	189
	Index	190

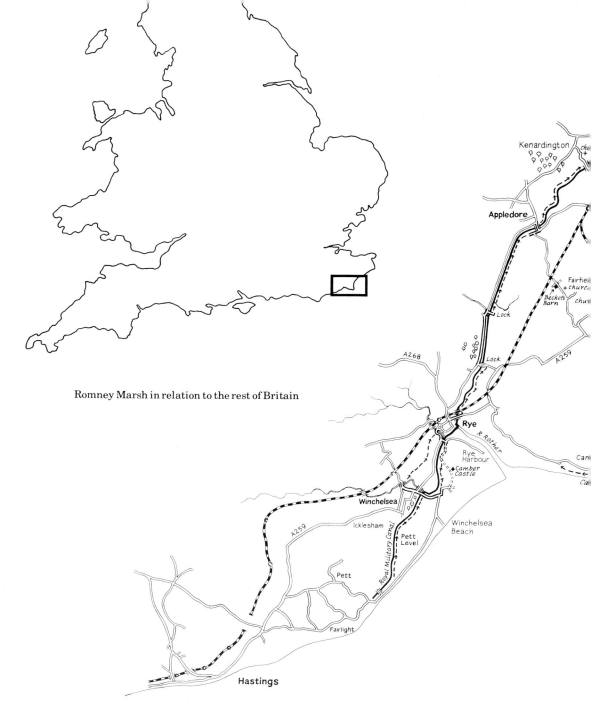
Romney Marsh in relation to the rest of Britain

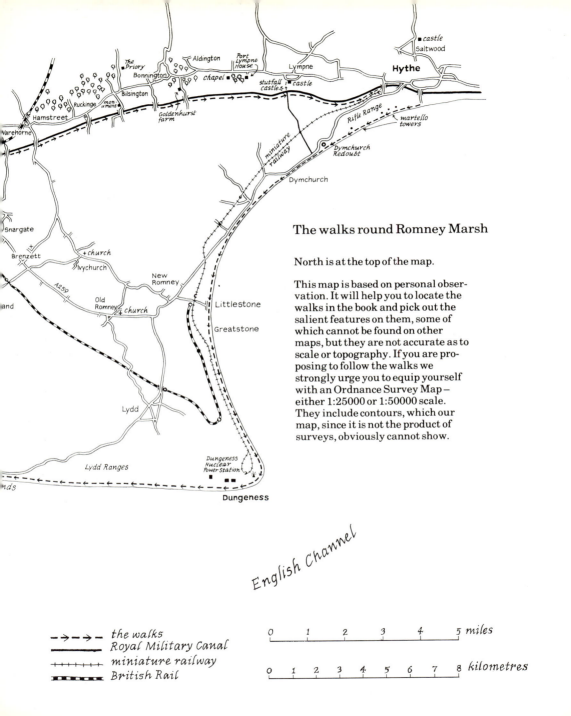

Introduction

When I started work on this book I went to see the artist and writer John Piper whose King Penguin *Romney Marsh* was published in 1950. Afterwards he wrote to me, 'I feel I didn't tell you anything about Romney Marsh, but I don't think I *know* much about it. What I really like about it is that it is all — 97% — atmosphere.'

If you go there you will immediately know what he means. A feeling of boundless space; a solemn stillness; a silence that is rare today in South-East England; flat fields covered with thousands of sheep and, even in the height of summer, a slight sense of eeriness.

Romney Marsh, as Piper explains in his book, is a generic term given to the area — about 50,000 acres in all — which is enclosed by the triangle Rye, Dungeness and Hythe. Today, apart from the maze of ditches and dykes which drain and dissect the fields, it is all solid land with the sea kept at bay by a number of barricades, like the huge sea walls at Dymchurch and Pett. But this was not always the case. At the time of the Romans the Marsh was more like a delta. The historian Nennius, writing in the ninth century AD, described an archipelago of precisely sixty islands each one surmounted by a rock, on which in each case was an eagle's nest. To the east the sea flowed up to Lympne (pronounced 'Lim'), where the Romans built their port, and the tide went up as far as Appledore along the present course of the Royal Military Canal. What happened next is still a matter of dispute. The Rhee Wall was built from Appledore to Greatstone along what was then the course of the Rother — some say by the Romans, others the Saxons, protecting the land to the east. In 1287 a tremendous storm diverted the River Rother to something like its present course, running into the sea, that is, at Rye.

With the help of natural processes like the movement of shingle and the silting up of rivers, wall and marsh, the area to the west of the Rhee Wall, was gradually reclaimed over the years by means of drainage schemes. In the twelfth and thirteenth centuries the kings of England established a system of elected Jurats to oversee the 'maintenance of sea walls and water courses for the common benefit and safety'. Even today a tax known as a 'scot' is levied from the inhabitants of the Marsh who benefit from the public drainage system. (Those who live on higher ground get off 'scot free' — hence the expression.) The improved drainage turned the Marsh into one of the finest bits of agricultural land in England. 'None but those who have seen it', wrote William Camden in 1586, 'can believe how rich the soil is, what great herds of cattle it feeds, which are driven here to fatten from the furthest part of England or with what art it is embanked against the sea.' Nothing much has happened since 1586 to alter that assessment, though with better drainage the quality of the soil has improved. The coastline has changed considerably but the look of the interior has not. Even the little town of Rye has preserved its appealing profile intact. Dungeness Power Station, with the inevitable line of pylons, remains the only blot on an otherwise ancient landscape. From the earliest times the area had been considered an Achilles Heel in England's defences. Edward the Confessor established the famous system of the Cinque ports. The original 'cinque' were Hastings, Romney, Hythe, Dover and Sandwich. (Winchelsea and Rye were included later.) Their duty, in the absence of a regular navy, was to provide ships for the defence of the south-east coast of England. In return for raising the ships the ports were granted a number of colourful privileges including soc and sac, tol and team, blodwit and fledwit, pillory and tumbrel, infangentheof and outfangentheof, mundbryce, and waives and strays. (Yarmouth was in addition granted den and strond, which led to a great deal of trouble.)*

At the time there was almost constant warfare with the French so the area is studded with castles— Lympne, Saltwood, Camber. Rye and Winchelsea are fortified with massive stone gates and towers. Both towns suffered badly from French assaults in the thirteenth and fourteenth centuries and Rye was three times sacked and burned.

Also surviving from the Middle Ages are a number of beautiful churches which, in spite of floods and flying bombs, remain in a state of fine preservation; almost all are well looked after.

The invention of the motor car has made most places accessible to anyone who wants to visit them. But, on the whole, motorists are conservative people who follow the herd. The Marsh has thus managed to retain its air of remoteness. Even so, anyone wishing to see it properly should travel on foot.

---

*1. *Soc and sac*: the right to hear all civil and criminal cases within their liberties. 2. *Tol and team*: the right of receiving tolls and the right of compelling a person found in possession of stolen property to name the person from whom he had received it. 3. *Blodwit and fledwit*: the right to punish shedders of blood and those who were seized in an attempt to escape from justice. 4. *Pillory and tumbrel*: mediaeval forms of punishment. 5. *Infangentheof and outfangentheof*: power to imprison and execute felons. 6. *Mundbryce*: the right to break into a man's *mund* or property in order to erect defences against the sea. 7. *Waives and strays*: the right to appropriate lost property or cattle not claimed within a year and a day. 8. *Den and strond*: the right to sell fish and dry nets on the strand free of charge.

Ministry of Defence permitting, it is possible to walk round the three sides of the triangle which bound the Marsh and this I have done—though not, I should say, at one go! On the whole the footpaths on the Marsh marked by the red dotted line on the Ordnance Survey map are poorly maintained, but it is generally safe to follow the tracks marked by the red symbol ↠.

In spite of its isolation the area is still well provided with public transport. There is a regular train service between Ashford and Rye with stops at Ham Street and Appledore, and buses serve most of the towns and villages, though in my own experience the posted timetable cannot be relied upon.

There are plenty of guide-books available and this is not intended as another one. An occasional visitor like me, making short forays usually in summer, cannot be expected to furnish the kind of definitive information available to the native. I have not tried to provide an exhaustive survey and have written only about the places and people that particularly interested me. I am very grateful to the authors of previously published books, a list of which is appended at the end of the book.

I would like to thank Tony Reavell of the Martello Bookshop, Rye, and Cliff Dean (both of whom made many helpful suggestions). In addition my thanks are due to the following for all their help: Annie Soudain, Alec Vidler, Dick and Phoebe Merricks, Sir John and Lady Winnifrith, Mr and Mrs William Deedes, Tom Pocock, Daniel Thorndike, Peggy Wright, John and Myfanwy Piper, Anne Roper, Dr. Trevor Beebee, Col. D.I.L. Beath, Mary Goldring, David Buchanan, the staff of the Imperial War Museum and, of course, Fay Godwin who roped me in and introduced me to the Marsh.

Part One

The stretch of the Royal Military Canal between Pett Level and Rye was the last section to be completed (in 1809) and because it has no navigable connection with the River Brede was not used by barges like the rest of the canal. It is much narrower and cannot be said to constitute a military obstacle.

Pett Level and the way to Rye

8813/8913

The road to Fairlight branches off to the right as you come out of Hastings on the Folkestone road. From Fairling, 450 feet above sea level, the road descends steeply to the coast, where the strange collection of holiday bungalows and cottages known as Pett Level clusters at the foot of the cliffs. Past the village store the road rounds a corner, and on the left there is a narrow canal which looks as if it is in danger of being stifled by reeds and rushes. You can walk along the sea wall, trying hard not to peer into the holiday houses which lie between the wall and the road, looking out instead over the sea where at low tide fishermen dig for lug-worm in the sand. Even in summer it is a peaceful place.

Opposite a cottage called 'Tamarisk', at the far end of the village, you will see a pillbox dating from the Second World War, the first of many military relics that lie littered all over this area. From across the channel the flat triangle, bounded by Rye, Dungeness and Folkestone, offers the most tempting place at which to invade England. At high tide the water at Dungeness is very deep, and inland there are few natural obstacles to stop an advancing army. Throughout history British governments threatened by invasion have done their best to put up barricades. Luckily, these systems have never been put to the test, so the various contraptions and devices have been left to linger on as picturesque relics of invasion scares that came to nothing.

The most impressive of these is the Royal Military Canal which runs for about twenty-three miles from Pett Level to Hythe. In 1803, following the collapse of the Peace of Amiens, Napoleon set his mind to the invasion of England. In and around Boulogne he began to construct an impressive flotilla of 1,500 barges in which he planned to ferry his troops across the channel. Advised by the defecting French general Charles Francois Dumouriez, the government of William Pitt began hurriedly to discuss ways and means of stopping the Emperor in his tracks. The original plan was to flood the whole area of the Romney Marsh by letting in the sea at selected points along the sea wall. The drawback was that it involved paying out large sums in compensation to farmers whose land would be damaged. Others favoured the construction all along the coast of the latest thing in fortification,

Martello towers. The canal was the brainchild of the Assistant Quartermaster-General Colonel John Brown (1756-1816), a Scottish engineer. His idea was to make an artificial barrier running along beneath the higher ground inland, which would stand in the way of an invader advancing from any point on the coast. Once built, it would cut off Romney Marsh in a neat triangle. The idea appealed to the Commander-in-Chief, the Duke of York, and on 26 September,

Pett Pools.

1804, William Pitt gave the go-ahead. The decision seems to have been taken swiftly, possibly as the result of a report that Pitt had just received from General Dumouriez in which the French defector pointed out how easily Napoleon could land his troops at Dungeness. At any rate the Duke of York gave orders that digging should begin at once. The canal was to run from the mouth of the Rother at Rye and was to be sixty feet across and nine feet deep. (Brown later altered these measurements to seventy feet and seven feet respectively.) Brown set out from London in October, 1804, to take charge of operations. He stopped at Sandgate to see General Sir John Moore, later the hero of Corunna, who was in charge of the

Pett Pools.

Spot the bird watcher (Cliff Dean) at Pett Pools

troops at Shorncliffe Camp, Folkestone. Unlike Brown and Pitt, the General did not take the idea of an invasion very seriously. 'I cannot be persuaded', he wrote, 'that Bonaparte will be mad enough to attempt it.' As for the British government — 'The experience of the last twelve months has taught me to place little confidence in the information or belief of ministers.'

Moore was to be proved right. Napoleon had at one time been so confident of his invasion scheme that he struck a special medal to commemorate the event with the inscription: 'Descente en Angleterre. Frappé a Londres. 1804.' On 15

Swans on Pett Level – about thirty pairs nest here every year.

Pett Pools. Formed when the earth was dug out to make the sea wall. Ornithologists have pumped water out to make conditions ideal for waders. Regular winged visitors include a couple of flamingoes.

August, his official birthday, he ordered a review of the invasion flotilla. While he distributed the medals to his soldiers, hundreds of barges, coming from their moorings all along the coast, would converge before him at Boulogne, striking fear into the hearts of British observers watching the scene from out in the channel through their telescopes. But the grand inspection did not proceed as planned. One of the barges collided with an obstruction and there was an undignified pile-up. The boats began to sink, soldiers were jumping overboard, bystanders were crying out in alarm— and all the time the British telescopes were trained on the scene. Napoleon was furious. 'He paced to and fro very

Camber Castle and water.

rapidly,' wrote Madame Junot, wife of the French general, 'and we could occasionally hear him utter some energetic expression indicative of his vexation.'

The following year, the year of Trafalgar, Napoleon changed his mind about an invasion and turned his attention to Austria. But by then the construction of the canal was already underway and, as usually happens with expensive government projects, the pressure to continue with the work in hand proved irresistible. For the next four years armies of navvies laboured away until eventually the canal was completed at a cost of £234,000. Though utterly worthless from the military point of view it acted, as it continues to do, as a

Improvised shelter on Pett Level.

useful drain for the marshland farmers, besides being a handsome and impressive project. Elm trees were planted on the northern bank and beyond them along the length of the canal ran the Military Road to allow swift access to troops, guns and supplies. Guardhouses had been built at every bridge, and commissioners were appointed to take charge of the canal. In 1807 they included the Commander-in-Chief, the Chancellor of the Exchequer, the Speaker of the House of Commons, and the Prime Minister. 'No canal in history,' writes Mr P.A.L. Vine in his book *The Royal Military Canal*, 'was ever controlled by so distinguished a body of men.'

It would be difficult to guess as you walk along the canal

895138

between Pett and Winchelsea that it had, originally, a military objective. By a white milestone on the main road a track leads invitingly along the bank beside the narrow silver strip of water. It takes you into a kind of fairyland: cattle and sheep graze; herons flap up as you approach and fly off lazily to a place of safety; swans drift in state down the little dykes and ditches that run into the canal. Towards the straight line of the sea wall on the horizon the huge green expanse of Pett Level stretches out dotted with sheep. Over the surface of the canal dragonflies hum and swallows swoop for food. There is a sense of enchantment which, when the weather is right, can be experienced anywhere on Romney Marsh. I can quite believe that strange things go on in this part of the world.

Grace Lovat Fraser, the sister of the artist and designer Lovat Fraser, who spent a holiday in Dymchurch in 1920, tells what I am sure is a true fairy story:

One day Lovat and I had an odd little experience on the Marsh. We were on a sketching expedition and had taken sandwiches with us. Suddenly we came onto a beautiful fenced field covered with lush grass. It looked very inviting and also rather odd for Marsh fields are seldom fenced, stunted hedges and dykes being more usual. We could see a few sheep and cows grazing and climbed over the fence to picnic in the field. As we did this, two large and, to us, unknown kinds of birds shot up from under our feet and circled over our heads before flying away. We were startled, for the grass hardly seemed long enough to have hidden them. Lovat began to sketch while I got out our lunch. One of the cows now walked over to us and breathed gently down our necks, then seeing Lovat's pencils and crayons laid on the grass, leaned over and pensively ate one or two. Lovat, terrified that it would be poisoned, tried to get them away but they were swallowed in spite of him while I grabbed up the rest. I have always loved sheep and wished they would be friendly so, as this seemed a funny sort of field, I called to two that were near us when to my surprise they walked over to me and lay down with their heads in my lap, where they remained until we had finished eating. Next day we tried to visit the field once more, but search as we might we could never find it again.

9017 Winchelsea sits above the canal on a little hill and the view of the village from Pett Level forms the background of Millais' famous painting *The Blind Girl*, now in the Tate Gallery. It is an immaculate place which could easily win the title of Best Kept Village In The World. The streets run parallel to one another dividing the houses into a grid system devised by Edward I on the principle of the French *bastides*. Grass verges are beautifully kept, fuchsias and hydrangeas are much

Winchelsea was at one time a centre of the wine trade with Bordeaux. Many houses have extensive cellars. An example can be seen at Manna Plat in Mill Road.

in evidence. Well-preserved women of fifty hover about with secateurs cutting the dead heads of their herbaceous plants. Unlike its neighbour Rye, Winchelsea has no vulgar antique stalls and few tea shops. The bus shelter must be the only unvandalized one in the district. The village has a peaceful and genteel air which makes the police station at the west end look rather superfluous. In the middle of Winchelsea stands a huge church, only a fragment of the original which was blitzed by marauding Frenchmen in the fourteenth century. There are some beautiful crusaders' tombs but the interior has been rather spoilt by the hideous stained glass designed in 1933 by Douglas Strachan whose pink and blue writhing forms suggest anatomical drawings of muscles and

A Winchelsea garden.

veins. Another designer of stained glass John Piper confessed to me that if the IRA were to give him one quite small bomb he would be happy to smash the whole lot in one tidy blast.

Coming out of Winchelsea by the old arched gate you can see Rye perched on its hill on the horizon. There are two ways of getting there on foot. One is to turn left at the bottom of the hill and take the footpath off to the right, which is signposted about a quarter of a mile along the Udimore road. This 'path' is typical of the many that are marked all over the Romney Marsh. What happens is that you set off confidently across a field scattering the sheep on either side and before long the

Strand Gate, overlooking the sea. The cottage was for a long time the home of actress Ellen Terry.

Crossing the dykes

path peters out and you find your way barred by a large ditch or 'sewer' as some of them are called— though they are not sewers in the conventional sense but merely drains. Somewhere there will be a plank to cross by, and you have to guess whether it will be better to turn left or right in order to find it. This process will have to be repeated several times before you reach your destination. If you like mazes and obstacle courses of an Alice in Wonderland type this can be fun. If not, a better

way to get to Rye is to walk down the main road to Winchelsea Beach— a bungalow development by the sea, as scruffy as Winchelsea proper is posh, complete with fish and chip shop and amusement arcade. Where the road bends sharply to the right, you carry straight on down a track marked to Camber Castle. Keeping to the left you come out on a wide grassy track along the bank of the River Brede. Camber Castle is on the right, a huge Tudor fortress looking

Martello Tower No 30, Rye. Built originally to protect the sluices of the Royal Military Canal and the rivers Brede and Tillingham. 'It was one of the very few towers that was not in some way fortified during World War II.'
Sheila Sutcliffe

Camber Castle. 'It was one of the five polygonal blockhouses built by Henry VIII for the defence of the South East Coast and was celebrated by Paul Nash in several beautiful water colours.' – *Shell Guide*
Nash lived at Dymchurch and also at Rye.

9120/9220

like a collection of giant elephants' feet which is, at the time of writing, indefinitely closed for repairs.

The track keeps close to the river and runs almost the whole way into Rye through sheep-filled fields. 'Rye, that wonderful inland island, crowned with a town as with a citadel like a hill in a medieval picture,' wrote G.K. Chesterton. From whichever direction you approach it, Rye looks inviting and hospitable, a fitting end to any journey. But it is especially pleasant to come into the town across the fields on foot for you get a sense of its antiquity and peace. Rye is almost unique among English towns in having escaped the plague of development. There have been no drastic alterations or additions to date, though at the time of writing there is ominous talk of a 'marina' at Rye Harbour and even an oil rig off the coast. The little streets have been preserved and, though a number of individual buildings like Lamb House or the Grammar School in the High Street stand out, it is more the combination of different houses and their intimacy that gives the town its special atmosphere. Wherever you are in Rye everything is within walking distance. It takes five minutes to walk from the station to the church at the top of the hill. Here is the prettiest spot in the town— Church Square— a miniature 'close' of charming cottages built round the ancient church and the graveyard; criss-crossed with paths among the tombstones and planted with a variety of beautiful trees and shrubs.

Rye from the tower of St Mary's Church. Ypres Tower and the River Rother, looking towards the sea.

River Brede from the tower of St Mary's church, looking towards Cliff End.

The skull of John Breads preserved in a gibbet cage in the Town Hall, Rye. Breads, a butcher, was hanged in 1743 for the murder of Allen Grebell. Grebell was the brother-in-law of James Lamb, Mayor of Rye, who fined Breads for using faulty weights in his butcher's shop. Breads decided to take his revenge but killed the wrong man by mistake as he was walking through the town wearing the mayoral cloak which his brother-in-law had lent to him. A note in the Town Hall says, 'The murderer's body was exposed in this cage for many years on Gibbet Marsh near Rye, the remainder of the bones being removed piecemeal by superstitious persons in the belief that the drinking of their infusion in water was a cure for rheumatism.'

Inevitably Rye is a tourist trap, and there is a steady stream of them, especially in the summer when the holiday-makers from Pontin's Camp at Camber flock into the town and wander about its narrow cobbled streets, peering from side to side like inquisitive penguins. In spite of all these incursions Rye has somehow managed to preserve, especially out of season, its discreet and cultured atmosphere. In winter or spring once the shops have shut a strange silence falls and you can hear footsteps in the street — a rare sound in a modern town. Meanwhile behind the touristy Rye — the antiques, fudge shops and cream teas — a reserved middle class is ensconced with a well-established round of poetry readings, bible meetings, music festivals and so forth, all of which would appeal to the town's most celebrated previous inhabitant, the American-born novelist Henry James (1843-1916).

You can visit his impressive Georgian home at Lamb House, now owned by the National Trust, but, for the 30p entrance fee, you only see over two oak-panelled rooms on the ground floor and into the garden— rather a raw deal. It is enough, however, to give you a whiff of this excessively fastidious, beautifully-mannered American bachelor.

Fisherman's cottage, Rye.

James was one of those writers who became 'a figure' in his life-time whom it was compulsory for any young, or for that matter old, Man of Letters to visit. Known as 'The Master' for reasons that are obscure he was paid court in his dignified Georgian house by almost all his contemporaries. Joseph Conrad and Ford Madox Ford walked from the cottage in Winchelsea where they were collaborating on novels. Kipling drove over from Burwash in his 1000-guinea motor car. H.G. Wells came from Sandgate, noting the Master's curious collection of hats:

On the table in his hall in Rye lay a number of caps and hats, each with its appropriate gloves and sticks, a tweed cap and a stout stick for the marsh, a soft comfortable deerstalker if he was to turn aside to the Golf Club, a light brown felt hat and a cane for a morning walk down to the harbour, a grey felt with a black band and a gold-headed cane of greater importance if afternoon calling in the town was afoot.

Other visitors took the train from London and walked up from the station to Lamb House where they were received by the master with unfailing politeness. 'In his search for the finest shades among the shadows of the past,' another visitor, G.K. Chesterton, wrote, 'one might have guessed that he would pick out that town from all towns and that house from all houses . . . I think in a way he really regarded himself as a

Boat building in Rye – one of many crafts that still flourishes in the town. Judd and Rowena Varley are building *Helping Hand*.

sort of steward or custodian of the mysteries and secrets of a great house . . . not without something of the oppressive delicacy of a highly cultured family butler.'

All those who met the Master tried to recapture his unique manner of talking. Chesterton wrote:

Henry James always spoke with an air which I can only call gracefully groping; that is not so much groping in the dark in blindness as groping in the light of bewilderment, through seeing too many avenues and obstacles. I would not compare it, in the unkind phrase of H.G. Wells, to an elephant trying to pick up a pea. But I agree that it was like something with a very sensitive and flexible proboscis, feeling its way through a forest of facts; to us often invisible facts.

After James's death in 1916 Lamb House was tenanted by the two Benson brothers, A.C., who in addition to some volumes of reminiscences and biography wrote the words of *Land of Hope and Glory*, and E.F., who used Rye as a setting for some very successful light novels, notably *Miss Mapp* and the *Lucia* series. Benson still has a big following and I found his books in print and on display in the Martello Bookshop in Rye's High Street. His description of Rye or Tilling as he called it is worth quoting, even if he missed a certain note of grimness in the little town:

There is not in all England a town so blatantly picturesque . . . nor one, for the lover of level marsh-land, of tall reedy dykes, of enormous sunsets and rims of blue sea on the horizon, with so fortunate an environment. The hill on which it is built rises steeply from the level land, and, crowned by the great grave church . . . positively consists of quaint corners, rough cast and timber cottages, and mellow Georgian fronts. Corners and quaintnesses, gems, glimpses and bits are an obsession with the artists. In consequence, during the summer months, not only did the majority of its inhabitants turn out into the cobbled ways with sketching blocks, canvasses and paint-boxes, but every morning brought into the town charabancs from neighbouring places loaded with passengers, many of whom joined the artistic residents, and you would have thought (until an inspection of their productions convinced you of the contrary) that some tremendous outburst of Art was rivalling the Italian renaissance.

Rye churchyard.

Church Square, Rye.

Rye still attracts artists, and their paintings and prints can be seen at the Art Gallery in the High Street. There are also four thriving potteries in the town of which the best known is the Rye Pottery, founded in 1869 and revived by Wally Cole after the Second World War. Their ware can be bought in a little shop called 'The Merrythought' opposite the main entrance of the church and the pottery itself in Ferry Road is open to the public.

Henry James's natural successor as Rye's most distinguished inhabitant is the Anglican theologian Alec Vidler who lives in Church Square. After a lifetime in the service of the

The Pump House.
A water reservoir built in 1735 to bring fresh water to the houses on top of the hill. In 1755 some calves feet were found in the water and the Rye citizens were told, 'Any persons who shall hereafter be discovered to throw any dirt, dust, soil, trash, nastiness or anything else into the reservoir will be prosecuted with the utmost severity.' In any case the people preferred to walk down to the pumps and bring their water up in buckets so the system was not used.

Church of England as priest, scholar, theologian, Dean of King's College, Cambridge, and Canon of St George's Chapel, Windsor, he has come back in his retirement to the house in which he was born in 1899. Built in 1236 it is the only stone house which survived the attack on Rye by the French in 1364. With his dignified air and long white beard Alec looks more like a Russian Orthodox patriarch than a Church of England priest. His family have lived in Rye since the seventeenth century and in 1820 his great grandfather started a career as a merchant and shipowner and soon built up a prosperous business. Alec, his father, his grand-father and his great-grandfather have all been mayors of Rye. He has every right therefore to be regarded as the *genius loci*.

Tourists, mistaking his house for a chapel or church, peer through its windows and sometimes even knock at the door.

Rye Market.

They may, if they are lucky, catch a glimpse of Alec pottering about the house humming hymn tunes to himself in the British Rail steward's jacket which he sometimes wears. The living room has huge black beams and above the fireplace a printed notice says 'Thank You for Not Smoking'. Below in his basket sits a disobedient Jack Russell terrier called Zadok. Anyone so rash as to park his car outside the Doctor's house will be taken aback to find the venerable theologian emerging to greet him with outstretched hand— 'How nice of you to come. But I don't remember inviting you.'

Part Two

Rye from the east.

Marsh and Canal to Hythe

Church of East Guldeford (sixteenth century). 'Decayed late nineteenth-century paintings cover the walls.' —*John Piper*

925206

To follow the course of the Royal Military Canal take the Folkestone road (A259) out of Rye and turn off onto a footpath to the left directly across the bridge over the Rother. This leads under the railway through a patch that can be muddy at high tide out onto a broad sheep track running along the elevated bank of the river. Once again you are in the marsh country among the sheep and also, here, you see various interesting wading birds which come to pick and peck about in the muddy river banks. The whole of the Romney Marsh area is a paradise for ornithologists being a kind of transit camp for birds flying in and out of Britain or just passing through. There is now an extensive nature reserve at Rye harbour where dozens of terns nest on the shingle in April; and near Pett Level are four pools which were formed when earth was dug out to build the sea-wall after the last war. Here the waders are for some reason exceptionally tame and can be watched at close quarters. At first glance these looked to me like so many little brown creatures of varying sizes pecking about in the mud. But with the help of a local ornithologist Cliff Dean, who lent me a pair of binoculars, I was soon able to distinguish spotted redshanks, ringed plovers and dunlins. The birdwatchers who stop here seem happy to exchange information but Cliff warned me of the ferocious spirit which now prevails among the more obsessive ornithologists who, like train spotters, collect 'sightings' of rare birds with the same manic persistence as any other

A condemned elm tree by the Royal Military Canal. They were Huntingdon Elms planted by the War Office in 1820. The wood was to be used for the making of 'muzzle loader' rifles. Almost all fell victim to the Dutch Elm Disease epidemic of the 1970's.

Pylons bringing power from
Dungeness.

collector. The arrival of a rare bird anywhere in Britain is quickly registered on the birdwatchers' grapevine and within a few days hordes of 'twitchers', as Cliff calls them, will turn up armed with expensive binoculars and cameras with telephoto lenses. At Rye Harbour he himself recently caught sight of a Little Bittern, a bird so shy that some frustrated 'twitchers' were not prepared to wait their turn to catch a glimpse of it and started throwing stones into the rushes to try to persuade it to emerge.

933226 A mile or so out of Rye you come to the first lock across the canal, where it is advisable to cross to the north side as the towpath to the south is very overgrown. It is a mile's walk
936244 to the next lock where the line of tall imported elm trees marks the divergence of the river and the beginning of the canal proper. Here the main features of Col. Brown's defence system are clear— the canal itself, the elevated bank

The Royal Military Canal near Appledore.

The canal is built on the Vauban system giving a zig-zag effect. The idea was to allow troops to fire laterally from the bank at an enemy crossing the canal lower down. You get the zig-zag effect driving down the Rye–Appledore road.

Kent Ditch boundary stone on the bank of the Royal Military Canal. Erected in 1806 it marks the boundary between Sussex and Kent.

'Ello? 'ello? 'ello? What's all this then?

Oast house near Stone.

Crowfoot on the canal.

The Marsh Frog (*Rana Ridibunda*). After establishing itself in Romney Marsh the frog has now spread to other places in South East England and is common in North Kent and on Pevensey and Lewes marshes. But it is only found in marsh/dyke systems.

Pillbox from the Second World War.

with the Military Road running along the north side, once covered with shingle but now, up to Appledore, tarmacked over.

There is a wide towpath to the south side which runs for three straight miles to the village of Appledore. The canal is now a decent width and the huge trees, which towards Hythe have died in such large quantities, here include species which have not been affected by disease, and these provide an impressive screen on the north bank. In summer the broad canal is covered with a carpet of kingcups and the banks are thick with loosestrife and flowering rush. A few impassive fishermen squat, patiently waiting for a bite. I could find little evidence of anything edible in the canal apart from a few eels and the odd pike, but the pleasure of fishing doesn't seem to have much to do with catching fish.

If there are few fish, there are plenty of frogs. The story goes that before the war an M.P. who lived near Stone was determined to do something about all the mosquitoes which infested his garden pond. (There were mosquitoes all over the Marsh in the old days and the inhabitants used to take quinine which stopped them getting malaria but made them very deaf instead.) He imported four pairs of Hungarian frogs which, finding the habitat to their liking, quickly multiplied until they had spread all over the Marsh. During the mating season in May, they set up an intolerable croaking noise but apart from this give little evidence of their presence in the landscape. However, they do come out and sun themselves on the banks of the canals and ditches. You can hear them plopping into the water as your footsteps approach. But it is very difficult to catch sight of one.

9529 Appledore is a handsome village with plenty of old red tiles and brick. It has a wide main street (unimaginatively called 'The Street'), an excellent pub for an overnight stay, 'The Swan', and a small mediaeval church.

966264 There is a minor road which goes south out of Appledore across the flat marsh country to nowhere in particular. About two miles along it, having crossed the railway line that runs between Ashford and Hastings, you see the little, red-brick, tiled church of Fairfield standing alone in the fields— looking like a Noah's Ark that has come to rest among the willow trees and the sheep. The church is kept locked and a huge key hangs outside the front door of Becket's Barn farmhouse nearby: anyone wanting to visit the church has only to collect it. There is no graveyard and the sheep graze right up to the brick walls of the church, leaving their droppings in the porch. The peaceful interior has untreated timber beams, white box pews and a three-decker pulpit. (The parish clerk sat in the low deck and the parson occupied the middle, going up to the top to preach his sermon.) Though seldom used, this

Appledore Church of SS Peter and Paul. Saplings have been planted by the National Trust to replace the diseased elms. The Trust has planted over two hundred trees, mostly oak and ash.

little church looks in no way neglected and there is a special sense of sanctity about it, both inside and out which is hard to describe. Perhaps it has something to do with the grazing sheep which lend a feeling of calm to any landscape. Sheep have always been treated as religious symbols, the single lamb symbolizing Christ and the flock of sheep mankind. They are placid, peaceful animals and when they have been sheared they shine in the sun, a spectacle beautifully described by Dorothy Wordsworth:

As I lay down on the grass I observed the glittering silver line on the backs of the sheep, owing to their situation respecting

The Church of St Thomas à Becket Fairfield. Rebuilt with great care in 1913 by W.D. Caröe, the church until recently, when local drainage was improved, was sometimes flooded and worshippers had to reach it by boat.

the sun, which made them look beautiful, but with something of strangeness, like animals of another kind, as if belonging to a more splendid world.

William Cobbett who looked at things with a less mystical eye observed the marshland sheep as he rode from Appledore to Hythe in 1823. They were, he wrote,

. . . very pretty and large. The wethers, when fat, weigh about

St Augustine, Brookland.

Shepherd's hut in winter, near Brookland.

twelve stone, or one hundred pounds. The faces of the sheep are white; and indeed the whole sheep is as white as a piece of writing paper. The wool does not look dirty and oily like that of other sheep.

These are 'Romney Marsh' or 'Kent' sheep, a famous indigenous breed, capable of putting up with keen spring winds and wetness under foot in winter. The quality of the Romney Marsh pasture has been famous for centuries. The geographer William Camden wrote in 1586 of the 'luxurious verdure . . . excellently adapted for fattening cattle'. Modern surveys have shown that the best pasture here will fatten from six to ten sheep per acre in the summer, and in some cases even more. Since the war when the sheep were evacuated much of the marshland has been ploughed up and planted with crops, vegetables, fruit and also, at Appledore, bulbs; but despite this change, the population of sheep has, with the better drainage of the soil, increased and the abiding impression is of a landscape stretching out into the distance covered with thousands upon thousands of sheep.

Fairfield is only one of several beautiful churches which are dotted over the Marsh. Almost all of them are decorated

Ham Mill, near Ham Street.

St Clement's Church, Old Romney. Much of the interior is Georgian with box pews and a minstrel's gallery.
'At this Old Romney there is a church fit to contain one thousand and five hundred people and there are for the people of the parish to live in, 22 or 23 houses!' – *William Cobbett*. Cobbett was convinced that churches like this proved his theory that the population in the Middle Ages had been larger than in the nineteenth century – a theory that he used to refute the 'birth controllers' of his day like Malthus.

035252

St Mary in the Marsh. Burial place of E. Nesbit, author of *The Railway Children*.

inside with oval-shaped black wooden boards from the eighteenth century on which texts from the Bible are inscribed in gold. Often the Ten Commandments, the Creed and the Lord's Prayer are to be found, as at Fairfield, on either side of the altar. Only a mile or two from Fairfield on the main Rye-Folkestone road is the much grander church of Brookland which keeps its bells in a detached belfry on the north side. This church too, like many marsh churches, has box pews. Sheep keep the churchyard grass in order. There is another example at Ivychurch, two miles away. Its pews have been removed and the interior seems empty in comparison with those of its sister churches, which are small and intimate. One of the most beautiful churches in England lies just off the Folkestone road at Old Romney. It is a thick chunky building guarded by an ancient yew tree, with text boards and box pews which are now painted pink thanks to a donation from the Rank Organisation which used the church when making a film of *Dr. Syn*, the famous smuggling story

St Mary, Kenardington. 'In its patched up state it has a certain charm but it is not remarkable.' – *Piper*

by Russell Thorndike who lived for a time along the road at Dymchurch.

Although the Government gave up control of the canal in 1877, it continued to hold on to the north bank on the parapet side until 1935 when it was put up for sale. The three-mile stretch between Appledore and Warehorne was bought by an Appledore resident Miss Dorothy Johnston who presented it

St Matthew, Warehorne.

to the National Trust. (Ironically only a few years after the sale the Government requisitioned the land when war broke out.) Thanks to the efforts of the Trust this is much the best kept stretch of the canal. Diseased elms have been felled and replaced with young saplings, though whether this will stop the rot spreading to the others remains to be seen. The old Military Road, now covered with grass and grazed by sheep, makes a very pleasant path on the north bank, though the view over the Marsh is at times screened by a thick hawthorn hedge which was also at one time part of the military deterrent. To the north you see the little church of Kenardington across the open fields. As John Piper says, wherever you go in Romney Marsh there is almost always a church in sight. The next to come into view is Warehorne. The road to the village, crossing the canal, marks the limit of the National Trust's property. The Rev. Richard Harris Barham, author of the *Ingoldsby Legends*, came here as a curate in 1817, later becoming Rector of Snargate— another marshland church just down the road. Like his contemporary William Cobbett, Barham took a satirical view of the Royal Military Canal:

975322

989325

When the late Mr Pitt was determined to keep out Buonaparte, and prevent his gaining a settlement in the county of Kent, among other ingenious devices adopted for that purpose, he caused to be constructed what was then and has ever since been conveniently termed a Military Canal. This is not a very practicable ditch, some thirty feet wide, and nearly nine feet deep, in the middle, extending from the town and port of Hythe to within a mile of the town and port of Rye, a distance of about twenty miles: and forming, as it were, the cord of a bow, the arc of which constitutes that remote fifth corner of the globe spoken of by travellers. Trivial objections to the plan were made at the time by cavillers; and an old gentleman of the neighbourhood who proposed as a cheap substitute to put down his cocked hat upon a pole was deservedly pooh-pooh'd down; in fact, the job, though rather an expensive one, was found to answer remark-

ably well. The French managed, indeed to scramble over the Rhine, and the Rhone, and other insignificant currents: but they never did or could pass Mr Pitt's 'Military Canal'.

Barham's son, in the memoir he wrote of his father, reminds us that Romney Marsh at that time 'abounded in desperadoes'. He tells how his father, walking home to his rectory across the Marsh would sometimes be accosted by

St Mary Magdalene, Ruckinge. Two fine Norman doorways on the exterior. The notorious Ransey smugglers are buried in the churchyard.

half-seen horsemen. Once identified, he would be allowed on his way with a cry of ' "Goodnight — it's only parson!" while a long and shadowy line of mounted smugglers each with his horse laden with tubs, filed silently by.' Just as it seemed the ideal place for invasion, Romney Marsh has always been a perfect spot for smugglers and has been ever since the first introduction of customs by Edward I. Even today the police keep a watch along the coast for illegal immigrants. In the early days the main smuggling trade was in the illegal export

Royal Military Canal at Bilsington with the Cosway monument and pylon.

of wool — an activity known as 'owling'. But when the government first began to put a tax on luxuries in the seventeenth century, smugglers began to import as well as export:

> *Brandy for the parson*
> *Baccy for the clerk*
> *Laces for a lady, letters for a spy . . .*

Throughout the seventeenth and eighteenth century gangs of smugglers fought running battles with coastguards and soldiers along the beaches and across the Marsh, while the general public, like Rev. Barham, nervously turned a blind eye, or even bought the contraband without any special qualms of conscience.

Dead elms near Warehorne.

Memories of the old smugglers still lingered on in the area and were recorded at the turn of the century by Ford Madox Ford (1873-1939), who eloped at the age of 21 with the seventeen-year-old daughter of an eminent chemist called Martindale who lived at Winchelsea. In 1894 the young Fords bought a cottage at Bonnington where they lived for two years, later moving to Pent Farm Aldington. Ford, a tall, blue-eyed man with a wispy moustache and double-chin was the grandson of the artist Ford Madox Brown and the son of a music critic. He was a brilliant journalist and editor with an unfailing curiosity about things and people and the ability to spot literary talent a mile off. He would sit in the editor's office at the *English Review* leafing through manuscripts, glancing at odd paragraphs, never reading a piece through from beginning to end. Once his eye lit on a short story called 'The Odour of Chrysanthemums'. The title itself struck him at once — 'Most people do not even know that chrysanthemums have an odour.' Ford read on:

The small locomotive, Number 4, came clanking, stumbling down from Selston with seven full wagons. It appeared round the corner with loud threats of speed but the colt that it startled from among the gorse, which still flickered indistinctly in the raw afternoon, outdistanced it in a canter. A woman walking up the railway line to Underwood, held her basket aside and watched the footplate of the engine advancing.

It was enough for Ford to recognize the hand of a genius and he wrote back at once to the lady signing herself 'E.T.' who had submitted the manuscript on behalf of a friend. The friend was D. H. Lawrence.

Ford himself wrote several books — novels, poems and memoirs. But one of his first books, written at Bonnington, was *The Cinque Ports*, which describes the country of the Romney Marsh in vivid detail. There were still villagers alive then who had themselves been smugglers and who remembered the famous Bourne Gang led by the Ransley brothers, who had had their headquarters at a cottage in the woods near Bilsington Priory and hired farm labourers for seven shillings a night to lead a horse laden with kegs of brandy from the coast. The Ransleys' methods were not unlike those of our own protection gangs — the Richardsons or the Krays. Ford learned in conversation with the old gaffers the sort of thing they did, for instance, to get the use of horses: a farmer who had bought three horses at Hythe market was leading them home when he was handed a note saying that they would be required at a particular spot on the coast the following night. Being new to the area he took no notice but some nights later he was woken up by the sound of

Riding on the north bank of the Canal, near Hythe.

his garden gate being thrown through his window and when he looked out he was greeted with a hail of bullets. 'After that,' says Ford, 'he lent his horses.'

025335   Further up the canal in Ruckinge churchyard a rough plank mounted on three iron supports marks the grave of two of the Ransleys who were hanged on Penenden Heath, Maidstone in 1800. Ford writes:

They say that years afterwards an old man returned from Australia to his native village. He lived until comparatively recently in the odour of sanctity, drew a small pension from th

Government, was liberal and generally respected. The population of the village turned out to a man to do honour to his funeral obsequies. It appeared afterwards that this venerable person was the informer who had hanged the old Bourne Gang, and that his modest pension was the Government's price for his treachery. The people who attended his funeral were nearly all children of the men in whose hanging he had had a hand.

St Augustine, Snave. The interior was restored by the Victorians.

Bonnington Church, dedicated to St Rumwold, Prince of Northumbria. 'Legend says that no sooner was the infant baptised than he at once spake and professed the Christian faith and died while still in his baptismal innocence." (Baring-Gould: *Lives of the Saints*)

The Royal Military Canal near Hythe.

All these stories Ford recorded from the memories of Bonnington villagers.

My informants have however [he added regretfully] nearly all died within the last few years. The hard winters and the hard times kill them off. They go, bitterly lamenting the old times. Those were the days. One old man — a mole-catcher by profession — affirmed that until he reached the age of thirty he had a pint of smuggled gin to his supper every day of his life.

From Warehorne Bridge to Hythe there is no continuous Right of Way marked on the map for anyone wishing to walk along the canal, but I have not found this a problem. It is best to stick to the towpath on the south side, though at Mill House, Ruckinge, and Bridge Farm, Bilsington, the way is barred by 'No Entry' signs. One can either risk the anger of the landowners or cross to the north side and walk along the old Military Road, now a thin strip of grazing land between the canal and the little 'back-drain' which runs parallel to it. Most farmers do not object to walkers so long as they behave sensibly and shut the gates.

St Eanswith, Brenzett. Interior
'Violently restored and refitted
in 1902.' –*Piper*

042341 A strange and crumbling obelisk is visible near the village of Bilsington. This turns out to be a memorial to Sir William Richard Cosway, a local landowner and campaigner for the 1832 Reform Bill, whose friends thought so highly of him that following his death in a coaching accident in 1835 they erected this incongruous monument which has survived despite being struck by lightning in 1967. Among Sir William's good deeds it is recorded that he helped some needy villagers to

105

Stutfall Castle. The remains of the Roman Fort which once stood on the sea shore. The walls are those of the garrison bath house and the *principia*, or garrison headquarters. Lympne Castle is on the hilltop behind (*right*).

Farm house near Lympne.

emigrate to America. At that time the fare from Rye Harbour to the United States was £8.

In addition to the curious Cosway monument Bilsington has a ruined priory once the home of Augustinian Friars and, later it seems, of a number of ghosts. At one time these included a woman who was murdered by her husband when she dropped a tray full of their best china, a monk who told a red hot rosary and a figure which, according to one witness who saw it sitting on a bed, 'was nothing but a large head with something scarlet hanging from the neck — something like a bunch of beetroots.'

Not surprisingly, in view of its rather desolate atmosphere, there are a number of ghost stories associated with Romney Marsh. Saltwood Castle has a haunted room and while Mrs Beecham was living at Lympne Castle she claimed to have seen a Roman soldier, a priest and an apparition which had the body of an eagle attached to the skull of a man and which was in the habit of flying around one of the castle bedrooms. Rye also has its fair quota of ghosts, as befits the home town of the author of *The Turn of the Screw*. A turkey cock, it is claimed, can sometimes be heard crowing in Turkey Cock Lane near the Land Gate, though according to one version the noise is made by the ghost of a friar who eloped with a nun and was subsequently punished by being bricked up in a wall and left to die. The remains of his monastery can be seen near the site of an excellent hotel-cum-restaurant called 'The Monastery' in the High Street. In the period 1958-60 the owners of the hotel, Mr and Mrs Young, were frequently disturbed by the ringing of the front doorbell in the middle of the night and more than once Mr Young saw what he described as 'a foggy appearance of a monk with a rather round face', though he never held a conversation with it. 'Never a conversation at all,' he said. 'He always rang the front doorbell and went on ringing until I acknowledged him with "All right, Charlie!" when he just grunted and that was all.' Ghostly monks have apparently been sighted many times in Rye, notably in Watchbell Street. The novelist E.F. Benson, who took an interest in psychic matters, describes how he was sitting in the garden of Lamb House with the vicar of Rye when he saw a man walk past the gate in the garden wall:

He was dressed in black and he wore a cape the right wing of which, as he passed, he threw across his chest, over his left shoulder. His head was turned away and I did not see his face. The glimpse I got of him was very short, for two steps took him past the open doorway. . . . Simultaneously the vicar jumped out of his chair, exclaiming 'Who on earth was that?' It was only a step to the open door and there, beyond, the garden lay, basking in the sun and empty of any human presence. He told me what he had seen; our visitor had worn hose, which I had not noticed.

Ghosts of a different kind hover about Goldenhurst Farm, Aldington, a mile or so from Bilsington. It was just an old seventeenth-century farmhouse when Noel Coward bought it in 1926. But he linked it up to a neighbouring barn which was converted on the ground floor into a blue and white library with a bedroom, dressing-room and bathroom for 'the Master' above. A huge new drawing room was added with two grand pianos, on which Coward used to improvise duets with Richard Rodgers and other musical friends — and an enormous sofa designed by Syrie Maugham. In this lavish hideaway Coward relaxed at weekends with his good-looking manager Jack Wilson and entertained his sparkling friends from London — Gertrude Lawrence, Binkie Beaumont and Rebecca West. Then on Monday he and his entourage drove back to London in a Rolls Royce filled with flowers from the garden. Living uneasily cheek by jowl with the Master's glittering circle were his parents and his Auntie Vida (his mother's sister). Coward was devoted to his mother, a small, very determined, little lady from Teddington and she returned his affection. But Mrs Coward found it hard to stomach her Micawberish husband Arthur, once a piano salesman who had preferred to spend his time sailing a model yacht on the pond on Clapham Common. 'You have never done anything to help anybody,' Mrs Coward remonstrated during one of their frequent quarrels at Goldenhurst,' and everything has been done for you. And yet you are so far from being ashamed of yourself that you plump yourself down on us, full of conceit, selfishness and self-appreciation and spoil our lives for us.' Arthur, a mild little man who wore a grey flannel suit, had to be kept at arms length from his sharp tempered wife and eventually the Master moved his father into a room over the garage. When not venting her spleen on her poor husband Mrs Coward would turn on her sister Vida, a smaller replica of herself in appearance. 'Vida should never have been here,' she told her son 'and now you will not find it easy to get her out of the house. She loves the luxury and the grandeur.' The animosity lasted till poor Vida died at the age of ninety-two. 'Doesn't she look pretty,' said Mrs Coward gazing at her sister in her coffin, 'just like a little snowdrop. It's a pity she looked so disagreeable when she was alive.'

Coward sold the farm in 1956 when he went to live in Bermuda for tax reasons.

As you approach Hythe along the towpath the land to the north rises quite steeply up towards Lympne. Near West Hythe a tributary canal runs off down to the sea and on the opposite bank there is a footpath running beside a stream up the hill to Lympne Castle. It passes by the huge chunks of Roman masonry littered about the fields and known by their Saxon name of Stutfall Castle. There is nothing much here to suggest either a castle or the Romans and the peaceful site above the Marsh, grazed by the ubiquitous sheep, has more of

Lympne (pronounced Lim) Castle. (Open all day every day July–September and on Bank Holidays.) Built in about 1360 the castle overlooks the marsh and the sea. There was a look-out for smugglers here, but it is also said that Lympne Church was used to store contraband, following the discovery of a secret cellar under one of the pews.

a prehistoric air like that of Avebury or Stonehenge. The Roman name of Lympne was Portus Lemanis — portus meaning a harbour — a reminder that at that time much of the area was covered by the sea.

Everyone who stays in Folkestone [H.G. Wells wrote in *Kipps*] *goes sooner or later to Lympne. The castle became a farmhouse and the farmhouse itself now ripe and venerable wears the walls of the castle as a little man wears a big man's coat. . . . You look down upon the sheep-dotted slopes to where beside the canal and under the trees the crumbled memories of Rome sleep for ever . . . Away below one's feet, almost at the bottom of the hill the Marsh begins and spreads and spreads in a mighty crescent that sweeps about the sea, the Marsh dotted with the church towers of forgotten and medieval towns, and breaking at last into the low blue hills by Winchelsea and Hastings; east hangs France between the sea and sky; and round the north, bounding the wide perspectives of farms and houses and woods, the Downs with their hangers and chalk pits sustain the passing shadows of the sailing clouds.*

Today Lympne Castle is only open to the public during the summer and people staying at Folkestone are more likely to go to its neighbour Port Lympne House where an equally spectacular view of the Marsh can be seen from the top of a flight of a hundred and twenty-five steps descending like a staircase of ancient Rome to the terrace of the house. The property was bought before the First World War by Sir Philip Sassoon, great grandson of David Sassoon a Sephardic Jew who in the days of Queen Victoria founded a vast trading and banking empire in Bombay. His sons gravitated to England and were smoothly absorbed into the aristocracy, thanks mainly to the patronage of the Prince of Wales who loved the company of wealthy Jews. Sir Philip (1888-1939), the third Baronet, was really a courtier in the old-fashioned sense. A millionaire at the age of twenty-three, a charming but restless bachelor — he played golf with two caddies to avoid the delay of a lost ball — he was keen to do anything in his power to assist the Establishment. Like his father he was elected Tory M.P. for Hythe. During the First War he became secretary to Sir Douglas Haig and in 1920 Lloyd George made him his P.P.S. Subsequently Sassoon served loyally under the Tories until his death in 1939. To the question of why this exotic amateur did so well in the political world Lord Beaverbrook succinctly replied 'Sir Philip Sassoon was a brilliant gossip and habitual flatterer. He had many houses and most capable chefs.'

Port Lympne was the most extraordinary of his three luxurious houses. The old manor-house on the site was transformed by the architect Sir Herbert Baker into a millionaire's fantasy *pied-à-terre* suitable for the Great Gatsby himself. The finished house, which contained a hundred rooms in all, enclosed a Moorish patio complete with six fountains, white marble pillars and blue-glazed tiles from Spain. The windows looking out into the courtyard were made of Tuscan alabaster an inch thick, the dining room was panelled with lapis lazuli. Murals were commissioned from some of the foremost artists of the day. Rex Whistler converted the billiard room into a wonderful *trompe l'oeil* tent with blue and gold tassels dangling from the ceiling and charming views of eighteenth-century London and Dublin.

In this exotic and unreal setting Sir Philip, wearing gold-monogrammed velvet slippers, played host to most of the famous figures of the twenties and thirties; the Prince of Wales and Mrs Simpson, Lawrence of Arabia, Noel Coward, Winston Churchill and Charlie Chaplin — a suite was specially redecorated in yellow and gold for his stay. All were more than happy to accept Sassoon's help and hospitality. 'When you are leaving for an unknown destination,' said Churchill, 'it is a good thing to attach a restaurant car at the tail of the train.'

Today Port Lympne belongs appropriately to an equally bizarre character in the shape of the zoologist and gambling club proprietor John Aspinall. He bought the estate in 1973 and converted it into a safari park and zoo with help from a number of friends like Sir James Goldsmith. (This was done against considerable local opposition; some members of the council fearing that elephant droppings would roll down the hill and pollute the Royal Military Canal.) Under Aspinall's supervision the Whistler mural has been restored and where Sassoon's celebrities sipped their cocktails there now stands an enormous black statue of a gorilla. Outside in the grounds much work has been done to retrieve the garden, once a

John Aspinall's black rhinoceros. 'We have found them to be intelligent and affectionate,' he says, reassuringly.

A public footpath through the Wild Life Park gives the walker a free view of the wild horses.

showpiece. The great border, 135 yards long, was twice dug over before replanting took place and the soil was enriched with 200 tons of elephant manure. (Port Lympne is open to the public every day of the year except for Christmas Day.)

A regular visitor to Lympne before the war as a guest of Sir

Saltwood Gatehouse and Moat.

Philip Sassoon, was the art historian Kenneth Clark — later to gain fame and a peerage following his highly successful series of TV lectures called 'Civilisation'. In his youth Clark rented a house from Sassoon opposite the gate of his drive, but at the outbreak of war, realizing percipiently that Hitler might well choose Romney Marsh as the best place at which to invade England, he moved to Gloucestershire. Ironically, in 1940 when Clark was working for the Ministry of Information he wrote a leaflet called *If the Invader Comes* which was distributed to millions of householders telling them what to do in case of emergency. Many years later in 1954 he learned that Saltwood Castle, only a few miles from Lympne, was for sale. He promptly bought it. The castle stands in the triangle between the A259 and the coast road to Sandgate. It is now, under the auspices of Lord Clark's son the Hon. Alan Clark

Saltwood Castle. The ruined Knights Hall *(left and below)* and Roman Tower *(below)*.

Tory M.P. for the Sutton Division of Plymouth, open to the public during the summer months. Its finest feature is the two towers at the entrance to the castle proper which are said to have been built by the famous fourteenth-century architect Henry Yevele.

In the Middle Ages the castle was an important and strategic place which in 1026 was handed over by King Canute to the

The Moat and North Wall *(left)*.
Thorpe's Tower *(below)*.

church and occupied from time to time by the Archbishops of Canterbury. But various lords and barons gained control and when Archbishop Thomas à Becket asked Henry II if he could have the castle back the king refused and installed a villain called Sir Ranulf de Broc who according to one report 'turned Saltwood into a den of thieves'. In 1170 the four knights who had volunteered to rid Henry of his 'turbulent priest' stayed at Saltwood before going on to Canterbury to commit their famous 'murder in the cathedral'. The castle was damaged by an earthquake in 1580 and in later years fell into disrepair. It was bought in 1794 by William Deedes M.P., scion of a famous Kentish family whose members have been prominent in public life for hundreds of years — a tradition still upheld today by Bill Deedes, ex-M.P., editor of the *Daily Telegraph* and former Tory minister who lives nearby at Aldington. It was his grandfather who started to refurbish the castle in the late nineteenth century and when Ford Madox Ford saw it in about 1900 he noted that 'it was so lately restored and converted into a dwelling house that it is still too white to take its real place in the landscape.'

Bill's father, W.H. Deedes, was a Christian Socialist who sold many of the family possessions, including the Castle. The bulk of the restoration work was done between the wars by Lady Lawson (later Conway), a wealthy American recluse whose first husband Mr Levi Lawson committed suicide after killing a boy in a car accident. Following his death she threw everything into the work of restoration — filling the castle with antique furnishings and employing a full-time stonemason whom she supervised in person from eight in the morning onwards. She restored the Archbishop's Hall of Audience as a memorial to her second husband Lord Conway, an archaeologist and mountaineer. This later became Lord Clark's library. 'I had always wanted to live in a Gothic house,' he wrote, '— perhaps some instinct left over from Winchester.'

The Chapel of Our Lady, Court-at-Street. Catholic visitors still cross themselves with water from the pool.

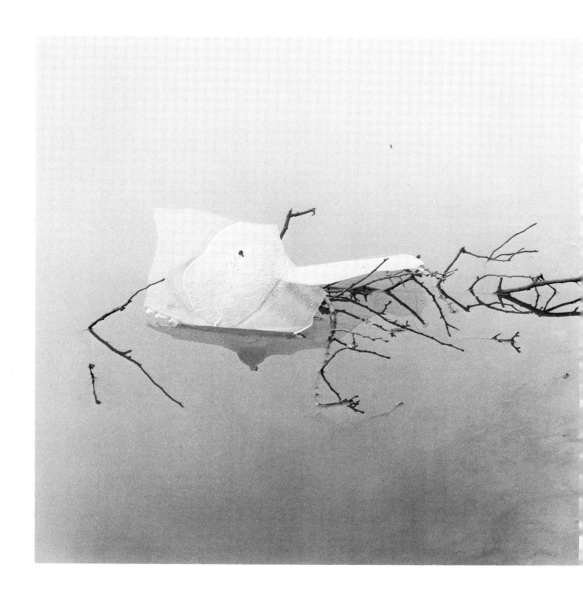

Another interesting mediaeval relic is to be found near Aldington in a field at Court-at-Street overlooking Romney Marsh, where stand the crumbling ruins of the Chapel of Our Lady, scene of a famous drama of the Middle Ages which is still argued about today. Elizabeth Barton (c.1506-1534), afterwards called the Holy Maid of Kent, was a servant girl in the household of Thomas Cobb, the Archbishop of Canterbury's farm manager who lived at Aldington. The girl suffered from some form of epilepsy and during her fits uttered prophecies and described visions of Heaven and Hell which greatly impressed her hearers. She was already famous and attracting pilgrims when she went to the Chapel of Our Lady and prayed for recovery from her illness. Later, attended by a huge crowd of pilgrims as well as commissioners appointed by the Archibishop of Canterbury to look into the claims made on her behalf she processed again to the chapel. There she apparently fell into a trance and was completely cured. Elizabeth Barton then became a Benedictine nun at St Sepulchre's, Canterbury. The following year, 1527, Henry VIII revealed his intention to divorce his first wife Queen Catherine and marry Anne Boleyn. At this point Elizabeth Barton told Archbishop Warham of Canterbury that 'God commanded her to say that if they married they should both be utterly destroyed'. Warham took her to Cardinal Wolsey who took her to Henry VIII and the simple servant girl from Aldington told her sovereign that 'if he married and took Anne to wife, the vengeance of God would plague him'. It is suggested that at a second interview with Henry VIII when she repeated her warnings he offered to make her an Abbess but she refused. In 1533 the king at last married Anne Boleyn and with the help of Thomas Cranmer embarked on a full-scale purge of those who opposed the match. The Holy Maid and a number of her supporters were examined by the Star Chamber, and she confessed to being an impostor. In April 1534 she was executed at Tyburn. 'The deceived people were well satisfied,' writes William Lambarde in his *Perambula-*

tion of Kente (1570), 'these daungerous deceivers were worthely executed and the Devill their Maister was quite and cleane confounded.'

Protestant tradition exemplified by Lambarde has upheld the idea of the Maid's spuriousness and the *Shell Guide to Kent* still speaks of her as a 'crazy servant girl'. Recently however the Catholic scholar Alan Neame has redressed the

Ancient churchyard wall at Hythe. The trees lining the old walls which wind up the hill like Tuscan lanes are ilex oak, an evergreen.

The Venetian Fête, Hythe. Held every other year it attracts thousands of visitors to the town.

1534/1634

balance in *The Holy Maid of Kent* (1971) a convincing defence of Elizabeth Barton which re-establishes her as a simple martyr for her faith and the subsequent victim of a crude propaganda campaign.

The remains of the maid's chapel, which were used to accommodate an army pillbox in 1940, stand in the private grounds of the Manor House, Aldington. Recently villagers have done much to clean up the ruins which, despite their dilapidated state, are still visited by Catholic pilgrims.

There is a Right of Way on both sides of the canal into Hythe. On the south bank a footpath runs alongside the miniature Romney Hythe and Dymchurch Railway and on the north there is a wider tree-lined bridleway. Once in the town of Hythe the canal becomes urban and respectable with tarmacked paths and park seats. Rowing boats are available for

The Church of St Michael's, Hythe, built in 1893.

hire. Every two years it is the setting for a Venetian fete, a celebration which began in 1860 as a feature of the Hythe Cricket Week. Thousands of people flock to Hythe and line the banks of the canal to watch a procession of incongruous floating tableaux pulled along by oarsmen in dinghies. In 1978, when I attended, the scenes portrayed ranged from the discovery of Paddington Bear to a very life-like representation of the Crucifixion.

Hythe has a busy, winding main street. To the north a number of lanes lead up to the quiet area which surrounds the handsome church. Children, who normally resent being dragged off to look at old buildings, will be fascinated by the crypt of Hythe Church. It contains about eight thousand thigh bones and two thousand skulls all neatly stacked in rows. It was traditionally held that they were the relics of those who had died in some great battle. This was the story remembered by George Borrow who at the age of four was taken by his mother to see the skulls:

St Leonard's Church, Hythe.

The greater part were lying in layers; some, however, were seen in confused and mouldering heaps, and two or three, which had perhaps rolled down from the rest, lay separately on the floor. 'Skulls, madam' said the sexton; 'skulls of the old Danes! Long ago they came pirating into these parts; and then there chanced a mighty shipwreck, for God was angry with them, and He sunk them; and their skulls, as they came ashore, were placed here as a memorial.'

Modern research suggests that the sexton's dramatic version of events had little historical basis. The skulls are not damaged as one would expect of the victims of a battle and they include those of several women and children. They are, however, thought to be foreigners, possibly the descendants of the original Roman settlers at Hythe, whose bodies were dug up during later burials and placed in the crypt in accordance with mediaeval practice.

Outside, the ranks of gravestones are stacked against the hillside and at the top of the churchyard you can sit and look down over the little town with its golf course, the huge four-star Imperial Hotel on the sea front and the rifle range to the west from which comes the ugly rattle of guns.

If the guns are not firing and the red flags are down you can walk along the shingle towards Dymchurch past the black fishing boats and the line of Martello towers which are dotted all along the coast in varying degrees of decay — though one on the front at Hythe has been successfully converted by an architect, Mr Ronald Ward, into a bijou residence. These towers, like the canal, formed a vital part of the anti-Napoleon fortifications. In their day they were the latest thing in defence. The inspiration came from an engagement between British and French troops in Corsica in 1793, when two British warships bristling with guns were held at bay by a mere thirty-eight Frenchmen occupying a tower at Mortell

Skulls in the crypt of Hythe Church.

Point — hence the name — armed with one 6– and two 18–pounder guns. Eventually the tower was captured from the land but even then only after two days of heavy fighting. The incident made a very strong impression on all the British officers present who included Sir John Moore. Captain Pakenham, an ancestor of our own Lord Longford, also witnessed this engagement. He later made a wooden model of the tower which was presented to the Royal Artillery.

Golf at Hythe. In the background, the Imperial Hotel.

Martello Tower No 13. Bought in 1960 by Mr Ronald Ward FRIBA designer of the new lighthouse at Dungeness. It has been lived in since 1928.

At the time of the Napoleonic invasion scare there was therefore a strong pressure group in favour of building a line of such towers on the South and South East coasts, at any point where the French were likely to land. In the end no less than 103 Martello's were erected between Aldeburgh in Suffolk and Seaford in Sussex. The standard design was in the shape of an upturned flower pot made of massive brick walls. An 18–pounder gun was mounted on top of the tower and two smaller ones inside, all intended to fire at ships offshore. The strength of the walls can be guaged from the fact that when Mr Ward was converting his tower on Hythe promenade it took two men, with a compressor and two guns, three weeks to make a wardrobe in his bedroom seven feet by seven feet by three feet.

As with the Royal Military Canal, by the time the towers were built the threat of the French invasion had long since receded. The work of construction, however, continued, much to the indignation of the Government's critics. In September 1823 the great journalist William Cobbett was in the process of making his famous Rural Rides:

I had baited my horse at New Romney and was coming jogging along very soberly, now looking at the sea, then looking at the cattle, then the corn, when, my eye, in swinging round, lighted upon a great round building, standing upon the beach. I had scarcely had time to think about what it could be, when twenty or thirty others, standing along the coast caught my eye; and, if anyone had been behind me, he might have heard me exclaim, in a voice that made my horse bound, 'The Martello Towers by —' Oh, Lord! To think that I should be destined to behold these monuments of the wisdom of Pitt and Dundas and Perceval! Good G— Here they are, piles of brick in a circular form about three hundred feet (guess) circumference at the base, about forty feet high, and about one hundred and fifty feet circumference at the top. There is a doorway, about midway up, in each, and each has two windows. Cannons were to be fired from the top of these things, in order to defend the country against the French Jacobins.

I think I have counted along here upwards of thirty of these ridiculous things, which, I dare say, cost five, perhaps ten thousand pounds each; and one of which was, I am told, sold on the coast of Sussex the other day for two hundred pounds! There is, they say, a chain of these things all the way to Hastings! I dare say they cost millions. But far indeed are these from being all, or half, or a quarter of all the squan-

derings along here. Hythe is half barracks; the hills are covered with barracks; and barracks most expensive, most squandering, fill up the side of the hill. Here is a canal (I crossed it at Appledore) made for the length of thirty miles (from Hythe in Kent to Rye, in Sussex) to keep out the French; for, those armies who had so often crossed the Rhine, and the Danube, were to be kept back by a canal, made by Pitt, thirty feet wide at the most! All along the coast there are works of some sort or another; incessant sinks of money; walls of immense dimensions; masses of stone brought and put into piles. Then you see some of the walls and buildings falling down; some that have never been finished. The whole thing, all taken together, looks as if a spell had been, all of a sudden, set upon the workmen; or in the words of the scripture, here is the 'desolation of abomination, standing in high places.

Since Cobbett's day the amount of abandoned military masonry has of course increased as a result of the 1939-45 war. In 1940 following the fall of France and the ignominious retreat of the British Expeditionary Force from Dunkirk, the logical step for Adolf Hitler was the invasion of England. Once again, as in the days of Napoleon, a flotilla of barges was assembled in the ports of Holland, Belgium and Germany, while the Führer with his generals and admirals pored over their maps debating the best means of putting 'Operation Sea-Lion', as it was code-named, into effect. After weeks of argument the decision was made to attack the South coast of England on a front stretching between Folkestone and Brighton. The crack 17th Division under General Herbert Loch was ordered to break through the coastal defences on 'Beach B' between Hythe and Dymchurch. Following the first waves of landing craft, amphibious tanks would crawl out of the sea, over the Dymchurch Wall and across Romney Marsh towards the Royal Military Canal. Resistance was expected here, but the German High Command anticipated that by the end of Day 1 of the invasion the army would have carried the line Paddlesworth-Postling-Sellindge.

This estimate was probably a realistic one. The defences along the South Coast were at that time far from adequate. When General Andrew Thorne was sent to Hythe in the spring of 1940 to take control of what was called XII Corps he found it consisted of only a few territorial units and a number of stevedores who were being taught how to drill with pickaxe handles. Later in the year the coastal defences in the Dymchurch area were taken over by the Somerset Light Infantry who dug themselves into slit trenches all along the sea wall and waited for the Germans with a meagre supply of Bren and Lewis guns. The Martello towers in Dymchurch finally came into their own and were manned with Vickers 303 machine guns. These were mounted on the tops of the towers from which the troops loosed off at low flying German bombers then coming in over the coast in their hundreds. To obstruct troops landing from barges a long line of scaffolding, booby trapped with mines, was erected on the sand. Inland on the Marsh, obstacles of every kind, including old cars, were brought out to stop gliders landing. A forest of poles was planted by troops to the irritation of the farmers. Pill boxes were erected along the Military Canal and at other rather randomly selected points— though it seems probable that like their predecessors the Martello towers many of them were put up after the real danger of invasion had passed. They still survive today along with the pyramidal chunks of concrete known as Dragon's Teeth originally sunk along those roads like 'The Street' at Appledore along which the Germans were expected to advance.

Meanwhile the boffins toyed with other more startling ideas like flooding the beach below the sea-wall with burning waste oil. Defence chiefs came down to watch the experiment but no-one was very impressed. As in 1805 there was talk, too, of flooding the whole marsh, but in the event only Pett

Level on the west side of Rye was flooded, much to the delight of a local ornithologist Mr Reginald Cooke who watched the arrival of hundreds of rare birds.

The situation in 1940 resembled in many ways the Napoleonic one. A loud-mouthed dictator stood on the other side of the channel breathing fire and slaughter while the British did their best to improvise a defence. And in the end, like Napoleon, Hitler called the whole thing off and turned his attention to Russia instead. Perhaps, after all, he had never had his heart in 'Sea-Lion'. For a start, he didn't like the sea; and then he clung to the belief that the British for whom he always had a love-hate feeling would somehow come to their senses and sue for peace.

In any case, after the Battle of Britain invasion was out of the question. Much of the Battle was fought over Romney Marsh and several German planes were shot down or crashed in the area. Some pilots who survived and were captured asked to be taken to the German HQ, having been told that Hitler was already in control. German planes and pilots are still today being unearthed. In 1973 a Messerschmitt 109, piloted by Leutnant Werner Knittel who was shot down at 5.10 p.m. on a foggy morning in October 1940, was dug up in a field at Burmarsh. The 39-year-old Luftwaffe pilot was still in the cockpit of the aircraft wearing his uniform and identity disc. Another Messerschmitt was excavated in 1974 at Melon Farm, Ivychurch, and the pilot's body nearby. Much of the recovery work has been done by David Buchanan of Tenterden, founder of the Aeronautical Museum at Brenzett where many relics of these aeroplanes can now be seen. (The museum is open every Sunday and Bank Holiday from Easter until October 31.)

Part Three

Looking towards Dymchurch,
with Martello Towers.

The shore to Dungeness and beyond

Dymchurch sea wall. A massive barrier over three miles long going back to the Romans. It was restored by John Rennie at the time of the Napoleonic invasion scare.

A rough two-mile walk along Hythe beach brings you to the ugly miniature fort that marks the limit of the army's rifle range. Here the Dymchurch sea wall begins and you can walk all the way along it to Littlestone. There has been some kind of wall protecting this bit of coast ever since the Roman occupation. But it was in 1803-4 that the foundations of the present massive barrier were constructed by the famous engineer John Rennie (1761-1821). Rennie who built Waterloo Bridge, Southwark Bridge and London Bridge, also played a major part in the construction of the Royal Military Canal.

Seeing the straggly mess of bungalows and holiday camps that constitute the modern Dymchurch it is hard to imagine what it was like at the turn of the century. 'It is small and white and very still,' Ford Madox Ford wrote in 1900, 'nestling beneath the shadow of the sea wall. It is as quiet as quiet can be.' In its day the village boasted quite an artistic colony which included the artist Paul Nash who was fascinated by the sea wall and painted it several times. Other regular visitors to Dymchurch were the Thorndike family, notably Russell Thorndike (1885-1972) the creator of Dr Syn and his sister, the actress Sybil. The children of a Rochester Canon, both had been stage-struck from childhood when they spent most of their time writing and acting in plays and charades of their own. It was while they were touring together in

America before the First World War that Russell conceived the character of Dr Syn. What happened was that one night a murder was committed outside the hotel in Spartanburg, Georgia, where they were staying. The corpse lay under their window all night. Sybil Thorndike was too frightened to sleep and while she brewed endless pots of tea, her brother tried to keep her spirits up with an extravagant fantasy about the man who had committed the murder, inventing there and then the character of the pirate-cum-parson Dr Syn, later transferring him in his imagination from the wilds of Georgia back to their holiday home at Dymchurch.

Thorndike wrote the book in the summer of 1914 in a coastguard cottage, while Sybil and her husband Lewis Casson occupied two houses in Marine Terrace just behind the sea wall. Though Russell was in his day an accomplished 'straight' actor who played Hamlet at the Old Vic and was the first English Peer Gynt, his natural bent was for the eccentric and macabre. He was a born story-teller who kept children entranced with tales of his adventures. Once, it was said, he queued up outside a theatre where he was performing and told the astonished box office man, 'I've come to watch this fellow Thorndike who they all say is so good.' He could roll his eyes and even, after years of practice, touch the tip of his nose with his tongue. No-one ever quite knew least of all himself where fact ended and fantasy began. 'Dymchurch under the Wall' and the Romney Marsh was the perfect place for him. He populated the Marsh in his imagination with smugglers and pirates — Dr Syn, Mr Mipps the Sexton, the doctor Sennacherib Pepper — a name that Thorndike borrowed from a Dymchurch tombstone — and Jerry Jerk the schoolboy who dreams day and night of becoming a hangman. The book was an immediate success and Thorndike later wrote six sequels — though as he had killed off Syn in the first book the others had to precede it in time. It was put on the stage with Thorndike playing the title part and has three times been made into

Martello Towers at Dymchurch. Tower No 24 has been restored by the Ministry of Works and is now open to the public. At Dymchurch, as at Camber, the sea wall acts as a barrier between man-made squalor and the unspoiled splendour of the sea. At low tide you have only to cross the wall to enter a different world.

a film, starring successively George Arliss, Peter Cushing and Patrick McGoohan. But the unworldly Thorndike failed to profit from his popularity — he sold the film rights for £20 which he spent in the Pier Hotel, Chelsea — and continued to tread the boards for the rest of his days, notably in the Open Air Theatre, Regents Park and for several years as Smee, the comic pirate in Peter Pan.

If Syn was almost a real historical figure to Thorndike it seems that other people have felt the same way. His name lives on in the lounge of the Mermaid Inn, Rye, and one of the engines on the Romney Hythe and Dymchurch railway is named after him. In 1963 the villagers of Dymchurch first

Dr Syn rides again at Dymchurch.

staged a fancy-dress pageant, which they called the 'Day of Syn', in aid of the church. It was such a success that it is now held every other year on August Bank Holiday. At 10 a.m. customs men and soldiers make their appearance on the sea wall — dragoons in scarlet coats, the press gang in stripe jerseys. They have heard that, 'there will be a run at 1.30.' Sure enough at half past one a flotilla of boats which has been standing by at Dymchurch make a triumphant landing on the beach and a procession of smugglers led by Dr Syn and followed by hundreds of holiday makers make their way to the recreation ground where a mammoth fête takes place, the proceeds going to local charities. On the Sunday prior to the Day of Syn there is a fancy dress service in the village church where all the helpers at the fête wear period costume — mob caps, silk waistcoats and buckled shoes. In 1977 Daniel Thorndike, who like his father is an actor and lives on the Romney Marsh, played the part of Syn in the pageant.

Another Dymchurch writer and a friend of the Thorndike family was Edith Nesbit, author of famous children's books like *The Railway Children* and *The Phoenix and the Carpet*. I always thought of her as a cosy respectable Edwardian lady and was surprised on reading Doris Langley Moore's biography to learn that E. Nesbit, as she was always known, was in her way a real Bohemian who led as turbulent a life as any modern feminist. She was seven months pregnant when she married Hubert Bland in 1880 at the age of 22. Bland was a radical firebrand with a monocle, one of the founders of the Fabian Society, and like many revolutionaries a compulsive womaniser. E. Nesbit, who became a keen attender at Socialist gathering, bore him several children and also brought up two children whom he sired by their housekeeper Alice Hoatson. She did not, it seems, resent her situation, being a genuinely tolerant and quite unconventional person by nature. When the Blands first established a holiday home in Dymchurch E. Nesbit, according to her biographer, startled the inhabitants by cycling along the sea wall in a billowing tea-gown and 'walking about arm-in-arm with the humble woman who did the housework'. Bland died in 1914 and with the outbreak of war E. Nesbit's fortunes declined. She was forced to sell her handsome house at Eltham and retire with her second husband a marine engineer called Thomas Tucker to a humble bungalow at Jesson St Mary's (now re-named St Mary's Bay) near Dymchurch. Here in 1924 she died and was buried at St Mary's in the Marsh, where a simple wooden board carved by her handyman husband marks the grave.

'The human span of life is far too short,' she wrote before her death, 'what things there are still to see and to do, and to think and to be, and to grow into and grow out of.'

It is appropriate that the home of *The Railway Children*'s author should lie along the route of the Romney Hythe and Dymchurch railway. This miniature line with its 15-inch gauge which runs between Hythe and Dungeness was the brainchild of yet another eccentric millionaire Capt. J.E.P. Howey (1887-1963). In 1837 Howey's father had bought a large plot of land in Australia for £128. When his son inherited it in 1924 it was the site of central Melbourne and Capt. Howey was therefore well able to afford to indulge his passion for model trains. The construction of the miniature

Lugworm diggers at Littlestone. Some diggers have been known to earn up to £80 a week from selling the bait.

The victorian Water Tower at Littlestone.

Bungalows at Greatstone. When New Romney was a sea port, Greatstone and Littlestone marked the arms of the harbour that enclosed it. The stones were navigational aids to sailors.

Playing fields at Lydd.

railway was begun in 1925, Howey working in collaboration with the engineer Henry Greenly. Although the original intention was to build the track along 8¼ miles between Hythe and New Romney — it was later extended to Dungeness. The project was completed in 1927 at a cost of about £110,000 (roughly £1½ million in contemporary money), and the line was officially opened by Lord Beauchamp the Warden of the Cinque Ports who remarked in his speech 'I am glad I have not been asked to drive the first train, as it would have resulted in the first accident.'

As a large (6'2") fully grown man I felt slightly self-conscious climbing into one of the handsome brown and cream carriages at Hythe station but I was relieved if surprised to find that the majority of my fellow passengers were also adult men, a lot of whom, it seems, never quite grow out of their boyhood fascination with railways, a fact which may explain why the Romney Hythe and Dymchurch line is still able to provide a regular hourly service during the summer season. Undoubtedly its finest hour was during the Second World War when the railway was requisitioned by the War Office to play its part in stemming the German Invasion. Romney Marsh has seen some fairly ludicrous defence systems in its day but none can have been more bizarre than the specially armoured toy train equipped with two Lewis guns and an anti-tank rifle which plied up and down the track manned by

149

the soldiers of the Somerset Light Infantry. To protect the train from German Air attack a camouflage 'hill' was built by Capt. Oliver Messel the well-known theatrical designer over a special siding near Dymchurch. It has been claimed that a German fighter was in fact shot down at New Romney by a corporal balancing a Lewis gun on the shoulder of one of his men. Later in the war the railway was used in the Pluto (Pipeline Under the Ocean) operation. The oil used by the allied D-Day Invasion troops was pumped under the Channel from a number of gutted bungalows in Lydd and the piping that was used was brought up on the train, while the station at New Romney was converted into a welding shop.

The atmosphere of 'Dad's Army' is strongly evoked from the wartime history of the area. On September 2, 1940, four German spies set off in a fishing boat from Le Touquet. Two of them were Dutchmen, one of whom had a Japanese mother and therefore a strongly Oriental appearance. They were arrested shortly after landing at Hythe. The other two came ashore in a dinghy at Dungeness but one of them aroused suspicion by trying to buy cider in a pub in Lydd at breakfast time the following morning. Three of the four spies were later hanged at Pentonville.

The beleaguered British might have been relieved to know that German intelligence about their defences was rather desultory. One Abwehr agent had reported on September 2, 1940, that 'the area Tunbridge Wells to Beachy Head, especially the small town of Rye (where there are large sand-hills . . . is distinguished by a special labyrinth of defences. . . . This area is extremely well guarded.' The reference to Tunbridge Wells lying thirty miles inland understandably mystified the Abwehr chiefs. They concluded that there must be two towns with that name, one of them on the coast, though mysteriously not marked on the map. The probable explanation was that the Post Office at the tiny village of Camber was then run by a Mr Tunbridge whose premises thus bore the sign:

TUNBRIDGE
POST OFFICE & STORES

Littlestone is conspicuous from the train or the sea wall on account of its lofty, castellated, red-brick water tower topped with a Union Jack which looms up over the village's famous golf course and its huge gloomy Victorian houses which look as if they are inhabited by lunatics or ghosts. At nearby Greatstone surrounded by acres of shingle there is a strange and unique erection known to residents as the Listening Post. It consists of a semi-circular concrete wall 200 feet long and about 25 feet high with another straight wall, two or three feet high about 150 feet in front of it. Until recently no-one really knew what it was. When I first heard about it, it was described to me as a 'Zeppelin detector.' Other people, apparently, thought it had something to do with coastguards and could pick up morse code signals from passing ships. In 1977 Lilian Madieson of Lydd was taking a friend on a guided tour of the area when she noticed that the 'Great Wall' was surrounded by water. A local firm was digging for gravel and it looked as if the familiar landmark might be in danger. Mrs Madieson immediately telephoned the Shepway Council only to be told by the Planning Officer that he could see nothing very special about an old concrete wall and was not prepared to do anything about it. Not being one to take no for an answer Mrs Madieson then got in touch with her M.P. and the Department of the Environment. The result was that in 1979 after a two year fight the D.o.E. eventually announced that with regard to 'Greatstone-on-Sea Listening devices' the 'above mentioned monument has now been scheduled'. Researches had in the meantime established that the 'wall' had been built in 1928 to detect aircraft within a certain height and distance range. It was one of only two such devices built, the other being in Malta and since destroyed. The

The unique listening post at Greatstone (left) with more modern 'saucers', which can also be seen in the cliffs near Hythe.

Greatstone 'thing' is now therefore unique. As with so many of the area's impressive relics I can find no evidence that it ever served any useful purpose.

The miniature railway runs on to Dungeness with mile after mile of bungalows blocking the view from the carriage windows. Here, and at Dungeness, there is a wide variety of those improvised dwelling places, like Peggotty's upturned boat, which sprang up at the sea side before the coming of planning regulations. Today the mass produced caravan is ubiquitous but in the twenties and thirties people who wanted a cheap home by the sea were allowed to be more adventurous and imaginative. Winchelsea Beach and Dungeness have several converted railway carriages which at one time could be bought from Southern Railways at Ashford for about £10 each, the price including delivery to the site. There are a couple of horse drawn buses at Winchelsea Beach ('Gladwin' and 'Caravelle'); 'Three Gates' is a tram and 'Robin's Nest' a green steel gasholder. Mr Brown at Toot Rock, Pett Level, lives in a converted gun emplacement which once housed a 6-inch gun bought from the Turkish navy by Britain in her hour of need.

Many of these exotic dwellings have equally exotic names. John Piper when he wrote his book on Romney Marsh included a collection of bungalow names which I append with a few additions of my own:

Hove To, Windy Cot, Midships, Galleons, Owl's Retreat, Ourden, Per Mart (Percy Martha perhaps), *Hildern* (Hilda-Ernest), *Karefree, Normaed* (Norma-Ed), *Sine Qua Non,*

Kasr-el-Nil

Robin's Nest   Samantha

The Willows

Mont Noel, Berylcot, Itsit, Cooparoo, Linga Longa, Kismet, Chequers, Sea Spray, Sea Close, Sea Wynd, Minarest, Thistledome (This'tle do me), *Twix Us, Emohruo* ('our home' backwards), *Ecnamor* ('romance' backwards), *Nelande* ('Edna Len' backwards.)

The most extraordinary and beautiful of all these seaside homes is the 'Shell House' belonging to Mrs Barnes at Win-

Mrs Barnes' Shell House

919171   chelsea Beach. Following the track to Camber Castle off the main Winchelsea-Rye Road you see a signpost pointing to a footpath across the fields on the right. The path crosses a stream or two and comes shortly to a wide dirt track. Turn right and you soon see on your right a quite remarkable sight — an ordinary little seaside bungalow, the walls of which are entirely covered with pictures made from thousands of sea shells. They are the work of Mrs Barnes, a Hungarian who

has lived here since 1970. The idea of decorating the house with shell pictures came to her out of the blue when she was sunbathing in her garden one day in 1977. 'My mind just seemed to fill with shells', she says. Once she started on the front of the house, fixing the shells onto a layer of polyfilla, friends, neighbours and local fishermen began to supply her with the shells she needed — scallops, mussels, razor shells and cockles. The pictures show local scenes and characters — Camber Castle, a shepherd with his sheep, Mrs Barnes' Alsatian Bambi, as well as a number of animals and birds. Most ambitious of all, covering one whole side of the house is a picture of a girl riding a mare with her foal. Every square inch of wall, including the coal bunker which has a design of squirrels, is covered with shells and the effect is not only beautiful but economic, as the shells help to insulate the building and save Mrs Barnes about a ton of coal each year. Since she is, quite naturally, proud of what is a unique example of 'primitive' art, Mrs Barnes is quite happy to show her work to visitors many of whom travel from far and wide to see it. 'Your house is like a paradise,' one of them told her. And it i

Dungeness beach. Fresh fish can usually be bought here and at many other places in the area. Contraband brandy and tobacco is also obtainable, it is said. Dungeness overlooks one of the busiest 'sea-lanes' in the world and because the water is so deep huge tankers can be seen at close range.

Dungeness Lifeboat. For many years it has been a family affair, with two families the Oillers and the Tarts to the fore. Lionel Lukin (1742–1834) 'inventor of the lifeboat' is buried in Hythe churchyard.

089169   Dungeness is the end of the line and has a strong feeling of the end of the world about it. The shacks and fishermen's huts, the two light-houses, old and new, are dwarfed by the huge blocks and cooling towers of the Nuclear Power station which gives off a rather sinister hum. The siting of the power station in a remote place like Dungeness must inevitably cast doubt on official reassurances that such constructions are perfectly safe. If so, why are they not built near towns like conventional stations? In fact, there are two power stations here – Dungeness 'A', built in 1965, was until recently supplying electricity into the grid via the ugly line of pylons

160

View from the old lighthouse with Romney Hythe and Dymchurch Station and track. The railway carries some 300,000 tourists every year. It also takes pupils to the comprehensive school at New Romney.

which straddles the Marsh. However after a mere fourteen years it has now, it seems, come to the end of its natural life and is due to be 'de-commissioned', or shut down. This follows a number of minor disasters, like the appearance of cracks in the cooling system and the concrete, caused in part by the very cold winter conditions of 1978-9. Despite these difficulties the Central Electricity Generating Board is still planning to build a replacement for Dungeness 'A', to be known as

Fishing at Dungeness.
The warm water drained into the
sea from the power station
attracts fish.

Dungeness 'C'. Meanwhile even greater problems have attended the construction of Dungeness 'B'. This too was commissioned in 1965 but it is still at the time of writing (1979) incomplete. The history of the project is one of astonishing chaos and incompetence. Even the Central Electricity Board now admits to 'straight-forward engineering idiocy'. The contract was initially awarded to Atomic Power Constructions, a British company that had no experience of

building power stations. Designs for the boiler system had to be rejected because of corrosion and fatigue, then the boiler system as a whole was scrapped and finally it was realized that no arrangements had been made for 'back-up cooling', now regarded as an essential feature of a power station of this kind. 16,000 workers were at one time employed to put things to rights. One group or another was continually on strike. In 1965 Atomic Power Constructions' original estimate had been £89m. By 1970 this had risen to £130m. In 1978 the C.E.G.B. who took over the project in 1970 were estimating that the final cost would be £344m, while the latest quoted figure has jumped to £414m, most of it to be borne, of course, by the taxpayer. Not surprisingly there is a strong body of opinion that thinks the whole thing should now be scrapped. It would be appropriate if the power station were to join all the other abandoned Government installations in the area and be allowed to fall into wrack and ruin.

arm near Dungeness.

Though to the layman like myself Dungeness looks like a dump, it is of great interest to a number of specialists. Geologists are fascinated by the way the tides and winds pile up the shingle, in such a way that the coast line extends gradually into the sea. You can tell how much it has shifted recently from the position of the old black lighthouse which is now well set back from the shore line, and the fact that a new lighthouse has had to be built. Fishermen come here, too, because the sea near the shingle is exceptionally deep— thirty five fathoms close to Dungeness itself— and so do birdwatchers. Much of the scrubby interior towards Lydd has amber Sands.

Camber Sands.

been designated a bird sanctuary, while the rest has been taken over by the Ministry of Defence who use it for firing off shells of various kinds. Red flags warn you when this is going on and you are then prevented from walking along the beach. I have been stopped near Camber by a menacing Dalek-like voice from a megaphone warning me to 'proceed no further'.

At Dungeness there seems no incentive to proceed further towards Camber except to get away as quickly as possible from the menacing blocks of the power station. This involves walking, usually into a fresh gale, along miles of shingle. Apparently the natives used to, and maybe still do, cover the ground on ski-like wooden boards. It seems hours before you put the power station finally behind you. Then gradually, if the tide is out, the shingle gives way to sand and you come out onto the great expanse of the Camber Sands. Old people often say that the Sands have been ruined by the coming of the huge Pontin's Holiday Camp, a sinister looking place surrounded by a high wire fence and notices warning you to keep

out, as if it was a prison and the campers convicts. The good thing is that from the sands the slope of the shingle and the sea wall shut off from view most of the squalid features of the camp and the rows and rows of caravans.

It is difficult not to walk out at low tide upon this famous beach without being uplifted by a sense of space and freedom, without feeling a childlike urge to take off shoes and socks

Church at Rye Harbour.

and run down onto the sand. The relatively few people who walk along it, the dogs and the ponies all seem insignificant and the passing human figure is quickly lost in the vast brown, grey and blue expanse of sand sea and sky which stretches westwards to the cliffs of Fairlight on the horizon.

Out of season on a winter or autumn afternoon, the beach is deserted. At such a time as I walk along the sands I begin to think sooner or later of returning in the dusk to Rye, preferably in a comfortable car, for a delicious if expensive cream tea in Fletcher's tea-shop which nestles near the church at the top of the hill.

Rye Harbour. The church was designed by S.S. Teulon in 1848. There is now a large nature reserve around the gravel pits.

Back to Pett. A picture Postscript.
There is a good walk from Rye Harbour, through the Nature Reserve and along the sea-wall to Pett. The wall divides the landscape from the seascape and the contrast between the two is always interesting.

Outfall for lowering the level of
Pett Level Lakes

Martello Tower No 28 at Rye Harbour. It was once known as the Enchantress Tower.

Ruined blockhouse.

Much of the beach at Pett consists of a prehistoric oak forest, which gives children muddy legs.

Groynes on Pett Beach, built following serious floods in 1926. Since the construction of the sea wall they have been considered redundant.

Visible at low tide on the Beach at Pett is the outline of the British warship *Anne* a 70-gun ship of the line lost in the battle of Beachy Head in 1690.

Shrimping at Cliff End.

Cliff End.

Bibliography

Ansel, Walter, *Hitler Confronts England*, Duke University Press, 1960.
Barham, Richard, *Ingoldsby Legends*, Everyman Publications, 1971.
Brenthall, Margaret, *The Cinque Ports and Romney Marsh*, John Gifford, 1972.
Camden, William, *Camden's Britannia: Kent* (edited by Gordon J. Copley), Hutchinson, 1972.
Chesterton, G.K., *Autobiography*, Hutchinson, 1936.
Clark, Sir Kenneth, *The Other Half*, John Murray, 1977.
Clark, Kenneth M. *Smuggling in Rye and District*, Rye Museum, 1977.
Cobbett William, *Rural Rides*, Penguin, 1967.
Davies, W.J.K., *The Romney Hythe and Dymchurch Railway*, David and Charles, 1975.
Fleming, Peter, *Invasion 1940*, Rupert Hart Davis, 1957.
Forman, Joan, *The Haunted South*, Robert Hale, 1978.
Green, R.D., *Soils Of Romney Marsh: Soil Survey of Great Britain Bulletin*, Rothhamstead Experimental Station, 1969.
Hueffer, Ford Madox (Ford Madox Ford), *The Cinque Ports*, Blackwood, 1900.
Hueffer, Ford Madox, *Memories and Impressions*, Penguin, 1979.
Hughes, Pennethorne, *Kent: A Shell Guide*, Faber, 1969.
Hyde, H. Montgomery, *Henry James at Home*, Methuen, 1969.
Jackson, Stanley, *The Sassoons*, Heinemann, 1968.
Lambarde, William, *Perambulation of Kente*, 1570.
Lesley, Cole, *The Life of Noel Coward*, Cape, 1976.
MacShane, Frand, *The Life and Work of Ford Madox Ford*, Horizon Press, 1965.
Mitchell, W.S., *East Sussex: A Shell Guide*, Faber, 1978.
Moore, Doris Langley, *E. Nesbit*, Ernest Benn, 1967.
Murray, Walter J.C., *Romney Marsh*, Robert Hale, 1953.
Neame, Alan, *The Holy Maid of Kent*, Hodder and Stoughton, 1971.
Piper, John, *Romney Marsh*, Penguin, 1950.
Sutcliffe, Sheila, *Martello Towers*, David and Charles, 1972.
Vidler, Alec, *Scenes from a Clerical Life*, Collins, 1977.
Vine, P.A.L., *The Royal Military Canal*, David and Charles, 1972.
Wells, H.G., *Kipps*, Cape, 1969.
Wells, H.G., *Experiment in Autobiography*, Cape, 1969.
Winnifrith, Sir J., *Appledore, Kent: A Short History*, (privately printed), 1973.

Index

Aeronautical museum, Brenzett, 137
Aldington, 122, 125; Goldenhurst Farm, 110; Pent Farm, 98
Appledore, 9, 74–5, 88; church, 75, 'Dragon's Teeth', 136
Arliss, George, 145
artists, 51
Aspinall, John, 116
Atomic Power Constructions, 168

Baker, Sir Herbert, 115
Barham, Rev. Richard Harris, 91, 92–3
Barnes, Mrs, 157–60
Barton, Elizabeth, 125–7
Battle of Britain, 137
Beaumont, Binkie, 110
Becket, Archbishop Thomas à, 122
Beecham, Mrs, 109
Benson, A.C., 49
Benson, E.F., 49–50, 110
Bilsington, 104, 105–9
bird sanctuary (Dungeness), 174
Bland, Hubert, 147
'Blind Girl, The' (Millais), 33
blodwit and fledwit, 10&n
Boleyn, Anne, 125
Bonnington, 98
Borrow, George, 128–30
Bourne Gang, 99–101
Brenzett aeronautical museum, 137

Broc, Sir Ranulf de, 122
Brookland church, 85
Brown, Colonel John, 17, 18
bungalow names, 153–7

Camber, 150–1; castle, 10, 40–1
Camber Sands, 175–8; Pontin's Holiday Camp, 175–7
Camden, William, 9, 81
Canute, King, 119
castles, 10; Camber, 10, 40–1; Lympne, 109, 111; Saltwood, 109, 118–22; Stutfall, 111
Chapel of Our Lady, Court-at-Street, 125–7
Chaplin, Charlie, 115
Chesterton, G.K., 41, 46–9
churches, 10, 82–8; Appledore, 75; Brookland, 85; Fairfield, 75–6, 85; Hythe, 128–30; Ivychurch, 85; Kenardington, 91; Old Romney, 85–8; Ruckinge, 100; Snargate, 91
Churchill, Winston, 115
Cinque Ports, 10
Clark, Hon. Alan, 118–19
Clark, Kenneth (*later* Lord Clark), 118, 122
coastal defences, *see* Martello Towers; Royal Military Canal
Cobb, Thomas, 125
Cobbett, William, 77–81, 134–5
Conrad, Joseph, 46
Conway (*formerly* Lawson;, Lady, 122
Conway, Lord, 122
Cooke, Reginald, 136–7

190

osway, Sir William Richard, 05–9
ourt-at-Street, 122–5
oward, Noel, 110–11, 115
ushing, Peter, 145

Day of Syn', 146
De Broc, Sir Ranulf, 122
Dean, Cliff, 59, 62
Deedes, Bill, 122
Deedes, William, 122
Dr. Syn, 141, 142–6; Rank organisation film, 85–8
Dragon's Teeth, 136
Dumouriez, Charles François, 6
Dungeness, 153, 160; nuclear power station, 160–8; shingle, 70
Dunkirk, 135
Dymchurch, 33, 88, 141–7; pageant, 145–6; sea-wall, 8, 41

Edward I, 93
Edward, Prince of Wales, 115

Fairfield Church, 75–6, 85
Fairlight, 15
Fishing, 74
Footpaths, 11
Ford, Ford Madox, 46, 98–104, 22, 141
Fraser, Grace Lovat, 33
Fraser, Lovat, 33
Frogs, 75

German invasion plans, 135
Ghosts, 109–10
Goldenhurst Farm, 110
Goldsmith, Sir James, 116
Greatstone, 151–2

Henry VIII, 125
Hoatson, Alice, 147
Holy Maid of Kent, 125–7
Howey, Captain J.E.P., 147–9
Hythe, 16, 104, 111, 127–30; beach, 141; church, 128–30

Infangentheof and Utfangentheof, 10&n

Ingoldsby Legends (Barham), 91
Ivychurch, 85

James, Henry, 46–9, 109
Jesson St Mary's (St Mary's Bay), 147
Johnston, Dorothy, 88–9
Junot, Madame, 29

Kenardington church, 91
Kipling, Rudyard, 46

Lamb House, 42, 46–9, 110
Lambarde, William, 125–6
'Land of Hope and Glory' (Benson), 49
Lawrence, D.H., 99
Lawrence, Gertrude, 110
Lawrence, T.E. (Lawrence of Arabia), 115
Lawson (*later* Conway), Lady, 122
Listening Post (Greatstone), 151–2
Littlestone, 151
Loch, General Herbert, 135
Longford, Lord, 132
Lydd, 174
Lympne, 8
Lympne Castle, 10, 111, 114; ghost, 109
Lympne House, 114–18

McGoohan, Patrick, 145
Madieson, Lilian, 151
Martello Point, 130–2
Martello Towers, 16–17, 130–5, 136
Maugham, Syrie, 110
Military Road, 30, 104
Mill House, 104
Miss Mapp (Benson), 49
Moore, Sir John, 18–22, 132
mosquitoes, 75
mundbryce, 10&n

Napoleon Bonaparte, 16, 18, 22–9
Nash, Paul, 141
National Trust, 91
nature reserve, Rye Harbour, 59

Neame, Alan, 126–7
Nennius (Roman historian), 8
Nesbit, Edith, 146–7
nuclear power station, Dungeness, 160–8

obelisk, Bilsington, 105
'Odour of Chrysanthemums' (Lawrence), 99
Old Romney church, 85–8
Operation Pluto, 150
Operation Sea-Lion, 135
ornithologists, 59–62

Pakenham, Captain, 132
Pent Farm, Aldington, 98
Pett, 8, 32
Pett Level, 15, 16, 153; bird-watching, 59; flooded, 136
Phoenix and the Carpet, The (Nesbit), 146
pillory and tumbrel, 10&n
Piper, John, 8, 91
Pitt, William, 16, 18
Pluto, Operation, 150
Pontin's Holiday Camp (Camber Sands), 175–7
Port Lympne House, 114–18
potteries, 51
power station, nuclear (Dungeness), 160–8
privileges, mediaeval, 10&n

Railway Children, The (Nesbit), 146, 147
Ransley brothers, 99–101
Rennie, John, 141
Rhee Wall, 9
Rodgers, Richard, 110
Romans, 8–9
Romney, Hythe and Dymchurch Railway, 127, 145, 147–52; as defence system, 149–50
Rother, River, 9, 18, 59
Royal Military Canal, 16–33, 59–128, 136, 141; Barham on, 91–2; locks, 62
Ruckinge, 104; churchyard, 100
Rye, 9, 36, 40, 41–59, 110, 178;

191

art gallery, 51; ghosts, 110, Grammar School, 42; Lamb House, 42, 46–9, 110; Mermaid Inn, 144; potteries, 51
Rye Harbour nature reserve, 59

St Mary's Bay (Jesson St Mary's), 147
Saltwood Castle, 109, 118–22
Sassoon, David, 114
Sassoon, Sir Philip, 114–15
'scot' (tax), 9
Sea-Lion operation, 135
'sewers', 38
sheep, 76–82
'Shell House', 157–60
Simpson, Wallis, 115

smugglers, 93–8, 99–104
Snargate church, 91
soc and sac, 10&n
spies, German, 150
Strachan, Douglas, 34
Stutfall Castle, 111

Thorndike, Daniel, 146
Thorndike, Russell, 88, 141–6
Thorndike, Dame Sybil, 141–6
Thorne, General Andrew, 136
tol and team, 10&n
Tunbridge, Mr (Camber postmaster), 150–1

Vidler, Alec, 51–5
Vine, P.A.L., 30

wading birds, 59
waives and strays, 10&n
Warehorne, 88
Warehorne Bridge, 104
Wells, H.G., 46, 49, 114
West, Rebecca, 110
Whistler, Rex, 115
Wilson, Jack, 110
Winchelsea, 32, 33–6
Winchelsea Beach, 40, 153; 'Shell House', 157–60
Wordsworth, Dorothy, 76–7

Yevele, Henry, 119

'Zeppelin detector', 151–2